THE

DAP

STRATEGY

DAP PUBLISHING

DAP Publishing Pte Ltd
24 Sin Ming Lane, #03-99, Singapore 573970
Inquiries@dapstrategist.com

ISBN: 978-981-18-1649-9 (print)
ISBN: 978-981-18-1648-2 (ebook)

Ordering Information:
Special discounts are available on quantity purchases by corporations, associations, and others. For details, contact Inquiries@dapstrategist.com

THE

DAP

STRATEGY

A NEW WAY OF WORKING
TO DE-RISK & ACCELERATE
YOUR DIGITAL TRANSFORMATION

RAJ SUNDARASON
FROM THE CHIEF EVANGELIST OF THE PIONEERS OF DIGITAL ADOPTION

CONTENTS

INTRODUCTION

By 2025, 70% of organizations will use digital adoption solutions
across the entire technology stack to overcome still insufficient
application user experiences.
—Gartner, technology analyst firm[1]

Predictions

It may be bold to begin a book with predictions of the future. But when the conditions for a tectonic shift in humanity arise, it lends itself to some crystal ball gazing. Before getting to my predictions, let's highlight these tectonic shifts:

1. The way humanity is leaning on technology is resulting in a new way of working, be it from home or the office or en route. Consumers of technology are demanding a shift in how they experience technology.

2. Digital transformation programs are a reality across most organizations around the world. It's this bias for change that has led organizations to commit vast amounts of resources in hopes of changing how consumers and employees engage with technology. For organizations, these transformations are a means of sur-

---

1   Melissa Hilbert and Stephen Emmott, "Improve Employee Usage, Engagement, and Productivity with Digital Adoption Solutions," Gartner Research, November 25, 2020, https://www.gartner.com/en/documents/3993544/improve-employee-usage-engagement-and-productivity-with-

1

viving and, in some cases, thriving.

3. By 2028, global software industry revenue will exceed $1 trillion.[2] This milestone will represent a watershed moment for us. Software will no longer be seen as a differentiator but rather as a staple. This will force us to rethink operating models so that business processes become liquid-like, simply flowing like water from a tap without friction or confusion. It simply works.

I believe in the power and potential of Digital Adoption Platforms (DAPs) to change the ways in which we work and live for the greater good. Of course, it's easy for me to be a believer. I've seen it happen time and again in organizations around the world and have experienced the impacts personally and professionally over the past five years.

My goal with this book is to share experiences, anecdotes, and thoughts about DAPs and their power to help enable and drive change. If at times I'm confrontational, it's because I want you to understand that for digital transformations to work, we need to embrace new ways of working; to challenge the norms and traditional approaches that are so ingrained in organizations today. The journey starts with the user, not the technology. To solve for the user will mean getting you closer to believing in DAPs too.

Today, organizations look to technology to solve for the disruption around them, the innovation they need to survive, and the transformation they need to thrive. The clever ones have learned from their flirtations with failure that, to improve their chances of success, they need a different approach in their digital transformation mindset. It will take a curious mind, one where the status quo is challenged almost daily.

This different approach is the DAP. The initial results from the past decade are encouraging, so much so that the leading analyst and global systems integrators are readying themselves for this next wave of DAP integrations. So far, we have seen wonderful stories where DAPs have impacted small clusters of humanity by making technology more accessible to users and resulting in better human outcomes. I will share some of these exam-

---

2   Neeraj Agrawal and Logan Bartlett, "Software 2019," Battery Ventures slideshow, May 2, 2019, https://www.slideshare.net/Battery_Ventures/software-2019.

ples in the book.

But first, some of my predictions—past, present, and future:

2020: *DAP is real and is mainstream*

By 2020, many of the Fortune 10, 100, and 500 organizations will be exposed to a DAP solution. These would be used in a point solution or departmental process mindset, not necessarily across the entire organization in 2020-21. If your organization is not yet on the journey, you may want to keep reading because more than 3,000 organizations have already begun the journey to DAP.[3]

2021: *Business & tech analyst firms legitimize DAP as a tech category*

Gartner issues their magic quadrant for DAP, following the Everest Peak matrix, which was published in 2020.[4] Other advisory firms follow suit with global system integrators building out practices to satisfy growing customer demand. Initially, the focus will be on content factories slowly evolving to provide a managed service around DAP analytics and advisory services for changes to an organization's operating model.

2022: *The DAP consultant becomes the new IT role*

Organizations begin to look for new skills to support DAP content curation and insights efforts around Digital Adoption Platforms. A new gig economy emerges for content curators. The DAP Consultant becomes the new business analyst as organizations battle with new disruptors to defend their traditional markets. The DAP Consultant job title sees tens of thousands of job ads on talent platforms like LinkedIn.

2023: *DAPs are a budget line item in most organizations*

With new success stories and a greater spotlight on the critical importance of DAPs in Digital Transformation programs, organizations acknowl-

---

3 Anil Vijayan, Sarath Hari N., and Rachita Mehrishi, "Digital Adoption Platform (DAP) Products PEAK Matrix® Assessment with Technology Vendor Landscape 2020," Everest Group, July 20, 2020, https://www2. everestgrp.com/reportaction/EGR-2020-24-R-3855/Marketing.

4 Ibid.

edge the need by including a budget line item dubbed "Digital Adoption" under the office of the Chief Financial Officer or Chief Transformation Officer tied to cashable benefits.

2024: *The DAP Center of Excellence emerges*

Organizations accept that they need in-house core competence around DAP across all facets of the organization. They start to think about organization restructuring to test out new operating models where core capabilities remain in-house and less critical functions like enablement and content build are right-shored to a content factory.

2025: *A Digital Adoption strategy becomes a core talent acquisition strategy*

Digital employee experience becomes a top five question on a candidate's decision criteria on whether to join the organization. Companies that do not have a legitimate answer will not merely struggle with first-day churn of new hires but will struggle to attract the right talent and skills because people will simply not want to come to work and put up with the complexity of work.

2026: *A Digital Adoption Index emerges*

Just like the Dow, a new index emerges that tracks the maturity of an organization's digital adoption against financial outcomes. The correlation will suggest that organizations with a higher return on adoption outperform the market and their industry peers.

2027: *The DAP dashboard becomes the pulse of an organization*

CEOs and CIOs will use insights from the DAP dashboard as a compass to the health of their digital transformation. It will be used to hold technology vendors accountable for the value being realized from the tech investments and value realization from DAPs will be tied to cashable benefits from de-risking, accelerating, and maximizing operational and financial metrics from digital transformation programs.

It will be interesting to see how many of these predictions hold true. I suspect that some may arrive sooner than expected. But the reality is that DAPs have arrived. Even more interesting will be witnessing how DAPs impact humanity in the decade to come.

CHAPTER 1

THE POWER OF HOW

I n September 2019, intense bushfires begun to rage in many parts of Australia.[5] Australians have become accustomed to the annual brushfire season that runs from roughly August through January. But due to a combination of unusually dry conditions and a lack of moisture in the soil, Australian authorities had alerted the public as early as June 2019 to prepare for an intense fire season.[6]

As it turned out, the 2019-20 season would prove to be catastrophic. So much so that it's come to be known colloquially as the Black Summer.[7]

Intense fires rampaged vast swaths of the landscape throughout the continent, burning more than 70,000 square miles and leaving immense destruction in their wake.[8]

More than 450 million reptiles, birds, and mammals were estimated to have died between September 2019 and January 2020 alone, according to

---

5   Lisa Richards and Nigel Brew, "2019-20 Australian Bushfires—Frequently Asked Questions: A Quick Guide," Parliament of Australia, March 12, 2020, https://www.aph.gov.au/About_Parliament/Parliamentary_ Departments/Parliamentary_Library/pubs/rp/rp1920/%20Quick_Guides/AustralianBushfires.

6   Andree Withey, "Bushfire Season Starts Early Across Northern Australia Due to Ongoing Hot, Dry Conditions," ABC News, June 26, 2019, https://www.abc.net.au/news/2019-06-27/bushfire-outlook-queensland-2019/11251150.

7   Tim Flannery, "Australia's 'Black Summer' Bushfires Showed the Impact of Human-Wrought Change," *The Guardian*, July 30, 2020, https://www.theguardian.com/environment/2020/jul/31/australias-black-summer-bushfires-showed-the-impact-of-human-wrought-change-aoe.

8   "2019-2020 Australian Bushfires," Center for Disaster Philanthropy, September 9, 2019, https:// disasterphilanthropy.org/disaster/2019-australian-wildfires/.

ecologists at the University of Sydney. The total estimated loss of animals was later revised to more than 1 billion.[9] It is likely that whole species of animals and plants may have been wiped out completely.[10]

The fires also damaged or destroyed more than 5,900 buildings and around 3,000 homes.[11] According to estimates from the Insurance Council of Australia, losses due to bushfires between November 2019 and February 2020 totaled more than $1 billion (USD) in insured claims.[12] That doesn't even take into account financial losses from the bushfires (lost income, reduced productivity) that are more difficult to tally. The Insurance Council of Australia, the country's main industry body, announced that as of March 2021 more than 25,600 insurance claims worth about $385 million (USD $395 million) had been lodged in 2021 (as of the end of March) as a result of the fires and floods.[13]

The effects of diminished air quality from the fires were felt around the world. Australians were unable to go about the normal routine of their lives due to breathability issues. At least 33 people lost their lives.[14]

In January 2020, help seemed to arrive in the form of rain showers. At first, the rains helped to quell some of the fire across the continent. But as the rains continued to fall, they became their own form of natural disaster.

The heavens opened up prodigiously. Some parts of Australia saw more rain in just a few days in January 2020 than in all of 2019.[15] Intense, continuous rains fell upon Australia, bringing immense, widespread flash flooding that resulted in yet more havoc in the form of property damage, power outages to more than 10,000 homes, and a muddy, fire ash runoff

9   "Australian Bushfires: Heavy Rains, Floods Provide Some Relief," DW Akademie, January 7, 2020, https://www.dw.com/en/australia-bushfires-heavy-rains-floods-provide-some-relief/a-52035739.

10 Richards and Brew, "2019-20 Australian Bushfires."

11 Ibid.

12 Tim McDonald, "Australia Fires: The Huge Economic Cost of Australia's Bushfires," BBC News, December 20, 2019, https://www.bbc.com/news/business-50862349.

13 Renju Jose, "Australians Assess Flood Damage, Accelerate Clean-up," Reuters, March 25, 2021, https://www.reuters.com/article/australia-weather/australians-assess-flood-damage-accelerate-clean-up-idINKBN2BI0IZ.

14 Richards and Brew, "2019-20 Australian Bushfires."

15 Mike Carlowicz, "Extreme Rain Douses Fires, Causes Floods in Australia," NASA Earth Observatory, accessed May 19, 2021, https://earthobservatory.nasa.gov/images/146284/extreme-rain-douses-fires-causes-floods-in-australia.

that spilled into rivers killing off untold numbers of fish.[16]

Then came the hailstorms. For a time, cricket ball-size hailstones pelted cities, towns, and the countryside throughout Australia.[17] There were also fire tornadoes. Some meteorologists suggested that the intense heat from the bushfires had created their own weather systems, leading to one type of storm after another.[18]

And though Australians had no way of knowing it at the time, a global pandemic was right around the corner.

You couldn't blame the average Australian for wondering if he or she saw the situation in more biblical terms, with themselves cast as a continent of modern-day Jobs.

Imagine for a moment that you're John or Jane Doe. Your life has been impacted forever in some cases. As a result of the hailstorms, you don't have a car to drive to work or to get your children to school because the windshield has been shattered. Imagine you have lost your home because it was destroyed by the bushfires. Or if your home managed to survive the blazes, it was rendered uninhabitable by floods.

You need the money from your insurance claim. In some cases, it represents a lifeline, a life preserver for many families; money to fix the family car that's critical for your livelihood. You need the insurance money to repair your house and shelter your family. But when you call your insurance company, you simply can't get through. You get a busy signal. Sometimes you get disconnected. At that moment, you feel helpless.

When you do manage to get through you wind up on hold listening to endless elevator music. Maybe, eventually, you get through. Most likely, you're greeted by a recording—a pleasant voice inviting you to leave a message but offering no time frame when you can expect to have your call returned. If you do actually reach a human, invariably you're put back on

16 "Australia Bushfires: Heavy Rains, Floods Provide Some Relief," DW, January 17, 2020, updated January 18, 2020, https://www.dw.com/en/australia-bushfires-heavy-rains-floods-provide-some-relief/a-52035739.

17 Jen Mills, "'Catastrophic' Hail Storm His [sic] Australia with Stones 'the Size of Cricket Balls,'" Metro, Monday 18, 2019, https://metro.co.uk/2019/11/18/catastrophic-hail-storm-australia-stones-size-cricket-balls-11177427/.

18 Sybilla Gross, "Climate Change Will Bring More Fire Tornadoes to Australia," Bloomberg, November 18, 2019, https://www.bloomberg.com/news/articles/2019-11-18/more-fire-tornadoes-to-hit-australia-as-climate-change-sets-in.

hold or transferred. More elevator music.

What you don't get is help from your insurance company when you need it most. It's not that your insurance company doesn't want to help. It's that they can't. They're paralyzed. They're struggling to manage the growing volume of calls.

Insurance claims due to fire, flooding, and hail in Australia soared in 2019-20.[19] There was not enough support staff to handle all the calls from desperate customers. Call times went up. Millions of people in Australia found themselves stranded, waiting for help.

We all know that basic business strategy suggests it makes good business sense to hedge your business risks. In this case, the insurance company would typically diversify its resource risk with a blend of off- and onshore resources. Not only does this facilitate the ability to scale its support needs, but the wage arbitrage makes perfect sense if the insurance company is trying to manage its cost-to-serve metrics.

Now, in any normal year this would have been a good decision for the insurance company to make. If not for the fact that right on the heels of the fires and the floods and the hail, the world was thrown into the chaos of the COVID-19 global pandemic.

The Philippines, a primary location for Australian companies to outsource customer service resources,[20] went into lockdown to curtail the spread of the virus in March 2020.[21] This severely limited the country's call center service industry's ability to step up and help Australian companies scale capacity economically to meet their customers' urgent needs.

It was in this historical moment, facing these difficult, compounding forces, that one Australian insurance company chose to rethink how they could rapidly bring new support center staff up to speed so they could be-

---

19   Terry Gangcuangco, "Revealed: Insurance Bill for 2019-20 Summer Catastrophes," Insurance Business Australia, May 30, 2020, https://www.insurancebusinessmag.com/au/news/breaking-news/revealed-insurance-bill-for-201920-summer-catastrophes-223760.aspx.

20   Heide Robson, interview with Mike O'Hagan, "44 | Offshoring to the Philippines," Tax Talks: Australia's Tax News Podcast, podcast audio, updated May 5, 2020, https://www.taxtalks.com.au/offshoring-to-the-philippines/.

21   Aie Balagtas See, "Rodrigo Duterte Is Using One of the World's Longest COVID-19 Lockdowns to Strengthen His Grip on the Philippines," the Washington Street Journal, March 15, 2021, https://time.com/5945616/covid-philippines-pandemic-lockdown/.

gin helping customers. The company would leverage technology, of course, but it's *how* they leveraged it that made the difference.

The insurance company didn't use technology to onboard or train the new support center operators—instead, they used a Digital Adoption Platform (DAP) to introduce their people to an entirely new way of working.

My Errors in Judgment and My Road to Digital Redemption

In the autumn of 2016, and after four years, I left SAP, the global German Software company that I hold dear to my heart to this day. In my time there, I had the privilege of representing this colossal brand initially across the Asia Pacific region and then in Southeast Asia. I was doing what I loved. I was in front of customers and prospects, evangelizing all that cloud software (more specifically cloud HR software) promised an organization to carry out its business strategy.

Before my time at SAP, I'd split seven years between Automatic Data Processing (ADP) and NorthgateArinso, Inc., delivering on business outcomes rather than merely selling software. My strengths were in front of a whiteboard, painting the art of the possible, and challenging senior leaders to think about the day in the life of their customers. I loved challenging executives to become more curious about their organizations, their business processes, and their people.

But even then, I knew all my experience would count for nothing if I didn't make a change. I had seen firsthand and had been complicit in perpetuating the problem. I was selling software without a clear understanding of how I would help the organizations buying the software realize the value of their investments. And the more software I sold, the bigger the problem I was helping to create. In my mind, we needed to sell *and* deliver on business outcomes, but we were falling short.

I realized that to be relevant in 2020 and beyond I needed to be part of the solution. And to be part of the solution—making technology deliver on its promise to companies and people—I needed to understand the problem firsthand. So, I did arguably the craziest thing I could do: I crossed over from being a software vendor to leading an HR digital transformation program for 26,000 employees across 13 countries at Bridgestone. It sounded glamorous at the time, but it didn't take long to realize how out of my depth I truly was.

I soon learned what a buyer deemed important during the buying process could be so fundamentally different from what a seller felt he needed to represent. The traditional pitch of the best product according to the most renowned analyst firm, the greatest number of certified consultants, the most completed implementations, etc., didn't really have much appeal when, as a customer, my focus was around cost, risk, compliance, and value realization. My company was in tire manufacturing, meaning that I needed to sell the idea of digital transformation to a bunch of executives and managers who were wondering why they should part with their hard-earned budgets on a promise of something magical.

It was during an oral presentation by Synchrony Global (now Rizing) that my life changed. Synchrony's president of human capital management of Asia Pacific, Mike Ellis, and his team actually listened to what we needed then led their presentation with a simple proposition:

"Let's do away with the traditional death by PowerPoint followed by the standard mind-numbing demo. Instead, how about we show you how you'll be using your future system?"

I have to admit this proposition was met with an uneasy silence in the room. Yet sheer intrigue had caught the attention of many in the room including Paul, the chief human resources officer.

"You mean, right now?" Paul asked. "With no training?"

Paul looked at me quizzically, wondering if this was a scene from *Punk'd*, as he looked for Ashton Kutcher to jump out from behind a screen.

"So, what do I do?" he asked, settling in front of a computer.

"Just follow the directions," Mike said.

In six quick minutes not only had Paul completed a process he had never seen before, but he'd done it accurately the first time. That Synchrony team won more than the hearts and minds of our company that day. They also won the business in the first 15 minutes of their pitch.

Synchrony had just successfully demonstrated how a DAP should be used at the front end of a sales to show how what they offered was different from the competition.

Unknowingly, that day Mike and his team launched me on my Digital Adoption journey.

Almost five years later, I have clocked over one million air miles on my way to consult with and for some of the largest brands, including Standard Chartered, Philip Morris International, Novartis, Nestlé, Orica, Globe Telecom, Ahold Delhaize, United Overseas Bank, Samsung, the Singapore government, and the list goes on.

I learned that the organizations that I have helped have two things in common:

1. Their digital transformations have failed to deliver on the value their suppliers promised and,

2. Regardless of language, geography, industry, or platforms, the problem was consistent globally; trying to get users to use the technology they had just implemented.

The key reason why they failed was not with the technology decisions they had made. The challenge has been the limited time they have spent focused on the user. Most of the time, organizations have blindly placed their trust in their technology suppliers and systems integrators without holding them accountable for measuring success in terms of digital adoption. That is akin to letting the fox not only into the henhouse but allowing it to set up shop there. For many organizations, the responsibility of ongoing value realization seems to stop at the hyper-care phase after launching new or updated software or processes. There are some that invest in application maintenance services contracts but none with a specific bent to ensuring business as usual (BAU) means users being able to use the digital tech stack in a consistent manner.

Since then, I have dedicated my life to better understanding this DAP journey. And I am pleased to share that it has been and continues to be an exhilarating, cerebrally challenging, emotionally packed adventure.

As I write this, I am the Chief Evangelist at WalkMe, pioneers in a market category called Digital Adoption Platforms (DAPs for short). Much of this book has been inspired by the platform WalkMe, which has afforded me the opportunity listen, learn and engage with many prospects and customers, colleagues, and analysts. These interactions have helped shaped this (my) point of view which I am hopeful will help others through their digital transformation journey.

What's a DAP? We'll dive into the specifics throughout this book, but the short answer is: DAPs successfully transform digital processes into digital experiences by putting the people who use technology at the center of the experience.

By "people" I mean new hires, experienced employees, vendors, and even customers. Anyone who will use your digital processes and technology.

But to put people "at the center of the experience," we first need to think of them a little differently.

We must think of everyone who uses technology as baby users.

Meet the Baby Technology User

To be clear, I didn't say *treat* technology users like babies. Instead, *think* of them as babies. Because that's essentially what all people are the first time they use software that's new to them, are, baby software users.

When babies are born, they know nothing. It's our job to teach them. To nurture their understanding of and comfort in the world into which we've introduced them. The same can be said for new hires, yet it extends far beyond new employees.

Any person who is new to using a piece or suite of software is a baby user. Maybe the person is new to the company and the software, as in the case of the Australian insurance company's new hires. But a baby user can also be someone who's a fixture at the company but they're being asked to learn a new piece of software or a set on new digital processes. Either way, the key to rapid adoption and success is in thinking of the users as babies and how best to help them learn to crawl, walk, and then run in their new world.

Ironically, most organizations do not look at their employees in these terms. They see a homogeneous stack of assets that might be of different shapes and sizes but certainly not in terms of technology savviness and capabilities. Without a rethink here, the risk is that employees never actually get out of the crawling or walking phase.

In the case of the Australian insurance company, they needed their new hire babies to grow up fast. As the company discovered—to the great benefit of its customers—it is entirely possible to help baby users go directly from crawling to running.

To accomplish this, the company turned to what technology analyst firms such as Gartner, Forrester, Constellation Research, and Frost and Sullivan are calling a DAP.

Bringing Up Babies

The seed for DAPs was planted a decade ago with a mother's curiosity about technology. Eyal Cohen's mother wanted to complete an online banking transaction but couldn't quite figure out how to do it. She called her son for help. She kept calling periodically over the course of a few months. Recognizing an opportunity, Eyal decided to explore if he could leverage technology to build a solution that could help other mums and dads who were struggling with the same digital process. His solution for mums and dads eventually evolved into the Digital Adoption Platform pioneered by WalkMe under the vision and stewardship of co-founders Rafael Sweary and Dan Adika.

Since then, DAPs have evolved exponentially in terms of scope and capabilities. Yet that original simple idea—helping people rapidly and easily navigate our digital world—remains at the core of DAPs.

Essentially, a DAP is a technology layer that sits on top of any digital (web or mobile) asset or software application used by the people at their company acting as a digital concierge or GPS to guide users through whichever software application they happen to be using.

To visualize what I'm talking about, imagine a rainbow cake. Even if you've never seen one, you get the idea that it's made up of layers of cake and each layer is a different color.

With a DAP, the first layer is made up of different systems across the company's enterprise. The next colored layer could be additional systems that have been purchased to plug the gaps in functionality that the original software can't cater for. Each cake layer has a sponginess, so think of the holes in the case as different silos that exist within the systems the company uses.

Then you've got the next layer, which contains all the business processes the people use those different systems for. Now imagine for a moment that many of these systems and processes are not connected. Here is where good intentions meet train wreck.

Where the richness of cream and cherries can be found on the top layer of the cake, we can also find the layer where the DAP interfaces with the baby users to guide them through all the processes.

A DAP is designed to make the software more human. It's always on the screen, discreet when not needed, yet right there just in time when you need it to be. Easily configurable and customizable for any application, the DAP engages and guides the user through the process.

It begins with the DAP proactively asking the user what task they want to complete then showing the baby user where to click if they need any concierge help onscreen. The DAP then guides the user through the software, indicating what the user needs to click or enter to complete the task, validating that they've entered the information correctly, ensuring they're in compliance with any internal or external standards, etc.

Once the user has completed the task, the DAP then ushers them to the next task to be done (if there is one) or reminding them of other tasks to be completed and helping the user complete those as well. At the end, it can even ask how the experience was, taking on crucial feedback that then filters into a chain of process improvement.

Because this guidance is so immediate and intuitive, a DAP allows even new users to quickly feel at home with unfamiliar software applications.

When the Australian insurance company's new customer service hires sat down in front of their computers on the first day on the job to process claims for the first time, there was no training.

Let me say that again: Their onboarding at day one was ZERO. There was no training on how to use the software to process claims.

Instead, when these baby users logged on to their application they were proactively engaged by the DAP. The DAP ushered them quickly through an orientation of the software. But instead of training the baby users how to use the applications, the DAP guided them through processes in real time: entering customer information, claim information, any internal codes required, and so on, all the while validating the data and ensuring the process was completed accurately and in the shortest possible time.

The insurance company was able to do this because one of the key features of a DAP is the ability to quickly build content designed to help your users through any process that's a part of their job. You simply map out what process and steps they will use, then quickly create content that guides, interacts, validates inputs, and tracks where friction sets appear as the user navigates through their job.

To be clear, with a DAP, we're talking about getting people *up and running on unfamiliar systems in minutes* as opposed to weeks or months. It's more about doing, not just learning.

Remember, a DAP does more than train someone to use systems. It's a new way of working that can aggregate information and present it to the user in the flow of work in a just-in-time manner. The user data tells us that users need a range of support assets to help them through a process. In the ensuing chapters we will discuss design principles that will help.

As soon as new hires at the Australian insurance company sat down to work, instead of them having to learn the software required to help process customer claims, they were doing the work as they used the tool. In short order, they had achieved mastery of those initial tasks and processes with very limited experience and in the process began to impact the business and some customer lives by reducing average call handling times.

Another way to think of a DAP is to think about the humble GPS. We have all used Waze or Google Maps to help us get from point A to point B. We plug in a destination, it understands where we are, and presents a set of instructions (turn left, turn right). Oops, you've missed the turn, please circle round. Be aware of the speed camera up ahead or please avoid the hard shoulder on the freeway as there is a stalled vehicle. These are what a DAP calls proactive intervention events of engagement. Simply put, you have a voice ready to poke you, helping you course correct.

Now I don't think anyone would suggest that a GPS teaches us how to drive, but I am sure we are all convinced of its value to navigate us safely and efficiently to our desired destination. This is what a DAP was conceived to do.

But the Australian insurance company's story doesn't end there. Executives figured that if a DAP could shorten the learning curve so dramatically for new hires, it would work for customers, too.

So, the company quickly created content aimed at converting a significant portion of their claims processes to self-serve claim files. This further reduced strain on their call center, and with no extra hiring costs. Using DAP, the Australian insurance company not only found a way to work faster to help meet their customers' needs, but they were also making fewer mistakes.

That is, their support staff was working faster *and* better.

Normally, call center employees experience lower job satisfaction during pressure-filled times. But the Australian insurance company's productivity flourished. Not only did cost-to-serve metrics begin to see improvement, but employee engagement and satisfaction began to edge up during this incredibly stressful time of natural disasters, pandemic, and increasing call volumes.

Why? Because they had been empowered by a DAP to use the tools they were given to reach the outcome desired by the company, the employees, and their policyholders.

In other words, the support team was experiencing the satisfaction we all feel from a job well done. And it's within that sense of satisfaction that lies the promise of all successful digital transformations.

Your company doesn't have to be facing cataclysmic natural disasters to realize the benefits of digital transformation through the use of a DAP. It can be something less lethal but no less of a challenge—consistently trying to be the best organization you can for your customers, employees, and owners.

CHAPTER 2

A GREAT MISUNDERSTANDING

W hat is "digital transformation?" In my experience, this is one of the most misunderstood business concepts in recent memory (right up there with "disruption").

Hear the term "digital transformation" thrown around during a strategy session and, if you're like most people, you nod your head at the vague idea and promise of the words.

Some people interpret it to mean the act of moving data and information into digital form rather than analog or paper-based media. But really, digitization is the better word for that.

To others, the words "digital transformation" may conjure images of entire companies or even industries in the act of using technology to become more efficient and profitable. In the paper, "Unlocking Success in Digital Transformations,"[22] McKinsey author Jean-François Martin shares that only 16 percent of respondents say their organizations' digital transformations have successfully improved performance and equipped them to sustain changes in the long term.

---

22 Jean-François Martin, "Unlocking Success in Digital Transformations," McKinsey & Company, October 2018, https://www.mckinsey.com/business-functions/organization/our-insights/unlocking-success-in-digital-transformations.

So just what, then, is "digital transformation?"

Simply put, it's the way those acts (digitization, digitalization) impact (transform) a person, a company, an industry, or even a society.

Act versus impact. This is an important distinction to make. So important, in fact, that it lies at the heart of why most digital transformations fall short of their grand promises of efficiency, cost-savings, and profitability.

This is also why the Australian insurance company *was* able to successfully revamp its operations to meet the needs of its Australian customers. They understood it wasn't about the tools. Instead, it was about rethinking how they thought about how their employees and new hires should use their tools.

It's not really about the process. It's about the *effects* of that process. We have seen many examples of this during the COVID-19 pandemic as nations grappled with the vaccination process. Many governments acted, but many others struggled to impact the vaccination process. Senior citizens across the United States and Canada have struggled to get vaccinated because they either don't have a computer or the digital experience to register for an appointment is beyond them.[23]

To give you a sense of the scale of the problem, over 22 million American seniors do not have broadband access.[24] In the York Region in Ontario, Canada, the problem is exacerbated by a lack of transportation or physical ability to travel for seniors to and from the vaccination centers.[25] This illustrates my point; many governments have acted but they haven't thought through the end-to-end journey of the process. They haven't thought about internet access, computer literacy, and being able to book safe transportation to and from the centers. These challenges are not confined to the

---

23 Kellen Browning, "Seniors Seeking Vaccines Have a Problem: They Can't Use the Internet," the *New York Times*, February 28, 2021, https://www.nytimes.com/2021/02/28/technology/seniors-vaccines-technology.html.

24 "Report: 22 Million U.S. Seniors Lack Broadband Internet Access; First Time Study Quantifies Digital Isolation of Older Americans as Pandemic Continues to Ravage Nation," *Business Wire*, January 27, 2021, https://www.businesswire.com/news/home/20210127005243/en/Report-22-Million-U.S.-Seniors-Lack-Broadband-Internet-Access-First-Time-Study-Quantifies-Digital-Isolation-of-Older-Americans-as-Pandemic-Continues-to-Ravage-Nation.

25 Lauren Pelley and Shanifa Nasser, "Use Mobile Vaccinations to Reach Ontario's 75,000 Homebound Seniors, Says COVID-19 Science Table," CBC, March 31, 2021, https://www.cbc.ca/news/canada/toronto/in-home-covid-19-vaccines-ontario-mobile-1.5971995.

developing world. For instance, Germany has also struggled.[26]

Enter Singapore. The city-state that you can drive around in 45 minutes with a population of 5.9 million (as of 2021).[27] The government started rethinking citizen services decades ago.

In 2018, they announced that all passports, national identification cards, requests for birth and death extracts, and applications for change of address would all be migrated online to support the Smart Nation goals. The processes account for 99 percent of transactions processed by the nation's Immigration and Checkpoints agency.[28]

In May of 2020, under the leadership of Minister S. Iswaran, Singapore announced the formation of the SG Digital Office (SDO), which is charged with the goal of bridging the digital gap between generations.[29] The mission of the SDO is to "mobilize a whole-of-nation movement to accelerate Singapore's digitalization by building on and ramping up existing efforts to equip every individual and business, including our seniors and small businesses, with digital tools and skills to participate meaningfully in the new social and economic environment post-COVID-19."[30]

In effect the minister was saying the nation was gearing up for a nationwide digital adoption strategy. No citizen would be left behind. When calls for vaccination registrations came, the process was simple: log-on to a portal and fill in five specific details:

1. Mobile number
2. Name
3. National ID number

---

26   Sabine Kinkartz, "COVID Vaccination: Germans Struggling to Get Appointments," DW, January 11, 2021, https://www.dw.com/en/covid-vaccination-germans-struggling-to-get-appointments/a-56195066.

27   "Singapore Population (LIVE)," Worldometer, accessed May 13, 2021, https://www.worldometers.info/world-population/singapore-population/.

28   Hariz Baharudin, "All Applications for Passport, NRIC to Go Online from 2020," *The Straits Times*, December 21, 2018, https://www.straitstimes.com/singapore/all-applications-for-passport-nric-to-go-online-from-2020.

29   "New SG Digital Office Established to Drive Digitalisation Movement," Infocomm Media Development Authority, May 31, 2020, updated June 22, 2020, https://www.imda.gov.sg/news-and-events/Media-Room/Media-Releases/2020/New-SG-Digital-Office-Established-to-Drive-Digitalisation-Movement.

30   "SG: Digital," SG Digital Office, accessed May 13, 2021, https://www.imda.gov.sg/infocomm-media-landscape/SG-Digital-Office.

4. Date of birth

5. Preferred language

Having gone through the process, I can attest that 99 percent of the experience is and can be experienced digitally—from the engagement of citizens, to the expression of interest to the booking of an appointment, to the logistics of transportation to and from the vaccination center to the registration and back home.[31]

While many Singaporeans have taken this simplicity for granted, others in different countries wish their digital experiences would be as simple, delightful, and effective.

You Say You Want a Revolution

Throughout human history, innovation has fueled a multitude of economic revolutions. Each of these economic revolutions has pushed human productivity—and humanity itself—forward.

Scholars have organized agricultural evolutions into three distinct buckets. The first focused on humans shifting from hunting and gathering to planting and growing healthier crops. The second agricultural revolution was fueled by improvements and acceleration of crop yields due to better practices like crop rotation, improved mechanization, and access to marketplaces as a result of the engine. The third agricultural revolution was driven by leveraging stimulants like pesticides and fertilizers, in addition to the ability to transport produce more effectively.[32] This evolution together with the emergence of marketplaces drove demand, which in turn fueled supply.

Ultimately, we witnessed a revolution in our agriculture that included advanced practices such as selective breeding to create heartier crops, crop

---

31   Mayuko Tani, "Singapore's Swift COVID Vaccinations Start with 5-Minute Bookings," Nikkei Asia, April 21, 2021, https://asia.nikkei.com/Spotlight/Coronavirus/COVID-vaccines/Singapore-s-swift-COVID-vaccinations-start-with-5-minute-bookings.

32   "AP Human Geography: Agriculture, Food Production, and Rural Land Use," Kaplan, accessed May 19, 2021, https://www.kaptest.com/study/ap-human-geography/ap-human-geography-agriculture-food-production-and-rural-land-use/.

rotation to maximize the soil, and more efficient and productive use of farmland to produce higher yields. These were the acts. The impact was the ability to better feed an expanding global population and get more from the land.

The 18th century saw our transition from a primarily rural, agrarian society to an urban society centered around manufacturing and industry. As what history now terms the Industrial Revolution emerged, the acts we witnessed were a major shift in our population centers along with a movement away from individual crafts work to mechanized production.[33] Commerce emerged. Outputs from the land became currency items resulting in a wealthier society with an increased production of consumer goods, not to mention the knock-on effects of climate change.

In the 20th century, with technology spreading and the demand for services growing, the world experienced yet another revolution with huge economic impact: the creation of the service industry.[34] More companies began offering services more than creating goods, placing huge pressures on these organizations to find the people with the necessary skills while also delivering a service at an affordable price.

While wage differences (cheaper labor) were an initial benefit for organizations that outsourced, we eventually began to see wage gaps narrow to the point that today the decision to offshore is now less one of cost and more about matching needs to capabilities.[35] These services have not only been driven by the growth of the middle class globally—especially in developing nations that offered a comparative advantage for services—but have resulted in establishing a middle class in those original developing nations. In the Philippines alone, the BPO industry contributes approximately $26 billion in revenue to the economy while employing in more than of 1.3 million citizens.[36]

---

33   "Industrial Revolution," History, accessed May 19, 2021, https://www.history.com/topics/industrial-revolution/industrial-revolution.

34   "Service industry," Britannica, accessed May 19, 2021, https://www.britannica.com/topic/service-industry.

35   "More Job Outsourcing, More Income Inequality," Public Citizen, accessed May 19, 2021, https://www.citizen.org/article/more-job-outsourcing-more-income-inequality/.

36   Lovie Antoinette, "The Future of the BPO Industry in the Philippines," CPW Outdoor Adventure, January 18, 2021, https://www.cpwoutdooradventure.com/the-future-of-the-bpo-industry-in-the-philippines/.

My point here is that revolutions are, in fact, good. They offer a new way of life, a different future, and the opportunity to truly impact humanity.

Now, here in the 21st century, I believe we find ourselves on the cusp of yet another revolution. This time it is tied to how companies are trying to leverage technology: it's a DAP-driven revolution. And, as with all the revolutions that came before it, this digital revolution is sweeping along not only business but society as a whole. I'm not just talking about the spread of digital technology. That's been going on for a while now.

What's more important to understand is the effect a DAP-driven revolution enables and the time impact that digital technology can have on us.

First and foremost, why do I think it's a revolution? Because we humans are spending a lot of money on it, because it is meant to drive profits, but more critically, because we are seeing how technology can make lives easier and because we have reached critical mass levels with more waves to come.

As projected by Battery Ventures in their report "Software 2019," written by Neeraj Agrawal and Logan Bartlett, global software spending will continue to accelerate and exceed $700 billion by 2021.[37] If that rate of spending continues at five percent annually, by the end of this decade organizations will have spent in excess of $1 trillion on software products.

But the burning question will be if all this software investment has been in vain and the biggest waste of money in the history of humanity? Or will it, as revolutions do, move humanity forward? Based on what I've witnessed firsthand over the past few years, Digital Adoption Platforms are the key to ensuring the digital revolution succeeds in moving us all forward.

I believe DAPs are about something more human than profits. DAPs are about the impact digital technology can have on humanity.

Doing What We Do Better

Ultimately, we all work to earn a decent wage to present a better future for our loved ones and family. Now imagine for a moment that I could

---

37   Neeraj Agarawal and Logan Bartlett, "Software 2019: IPOs, M&A, and Forces of Growth – Here's Software 2019," Battery, May 2, 2019, https://www.slideshare.net/Battery_Ventures/software-2019?ref=https://www.battery.com/.

offer you a mechanism that helped your employees better execute on their corporate goals, resulting in a better outcome for the organization.

This should result in better profits and in turn lead to a better share price and, most critically, a better bonus for the employee—a bonus that could be used for better healthcare, better education, and perhaps an improved living situation.

Add to that the ability to dial back pressures, mental health challenges, and frustration in the workplace. This is the core essence of what a Digital Adoption Platform is designed to do: impact humanity positively.

I believe the world we live in today has three movements that are upon us and driving change. The first is the democratization of information (access and publication).

The second relates to the impacts of COVID-19, namely changed priorities around things like working from home (how much and for how long remains to be seen, but the way we see work has been altered).

But it is the third movement that promises the most. There is a movement of equity that is being driven by the generation to come en masse and supported by the disenfranchised at large.

When you see the impact young activists like Greta Thunberg, the Swedish climate activist, have had on this generation and the generation to come with her views on climate change you can see how causes can impact change.

We have seen how Black Lives Matter can unite the globe to stand up to simply unacceptable behavior, shifting the conversation of diversity from a statistical point to one where the world is realizing that this needs to be part of the corporate narrative. Diversity of thought needs to be at the core DNA to drive equity within society.

Technology is not only empowering the world to learn and craft points of view, it has also provided people with the platforms from which to be heard. Generation Z values trust, and the trustworthiness of an employer or brand will determine if it warrants their commitment to working there or supporting their goods or services. It would take a brave man or woman to bet against these movements.

In April 2020, during Microsoft's second quarter earnings announcement, CEO Satya Nadella shared that one of the things COVID-19 did for us was to accelerate digital transformation out of necessity. "We have seen two years' worth of digital transformation in two months.... There is both immediate surge demand and systemic cultural changes…that will define the way we live and work going forward."[38]

People, both experienced workers and new hires, were forced to learn a new way of doing their jobs.

Again, pleasant or not, all revolutions move humanity forward. It's early in our current revolution, but it seems that with the aid of DAPs, baby users will be able to improve quickly, be more productive, more engaged, and more inspired to take on the challenges because they are more confident technology users thanks to the use of DAPs.

So how do you and your organization measure the success—the impact—of this transformative digital revolution within your organization?

You have to ask yourself: Is my organization a caterpillar? That is, before you started your transformation, your organization was a caterpillar. Is it a butterfly now?

Remember, it's about the *effects* of that process. Or more simply stated, do your efforts toward a digital transformation give you your desired outcome? This is not only the measure of a successful digital transformation; *it is the key to understanding how to achieve success no matter the scale.*

So, have you achieved butterfly status? Or are you still wrapped in your cocoon? Are you still that furry caterpillar crawling across a leaf, maybe with some new spots and color? Or is your metamorphosis so clear and apparent you can see the new crisp wings of the butterfly fully functioning as you and your team flies effortlessly across the noise of disruption?

---

38   "Microsoft Corp (MSFT) CEO Satya Nadella on Q3 2020 Results—Earnings Call Transcript," Seeking Alpha, April 29, 2020, https://seekingalpha.com/article/4341291-microsoft-corp-msft-ceo-satya-nadella-on-q3-2020-results-earnings-call-transcript?part=single.

How a Caterpillar Turns into a Butterfly... and Why It Matters

The caterpillar's metamorphosis from a tree clinging, 12-legged pest into a fluttering, majestic butterfly is often used as a metaphor for digital transformations. While the result of the process comes across as magnificent, the process taking place deep inside the chrysalis is, in fact, a pretty gruesome sight.

Trust me, this is how many digital transformations start and end up. And in both cases, it's a fascinating journey from one state of being to another with key markers along the way.

For a caterpillar to transform it needs to digest itself, essentially turning itself into a protein-rich soup.[39] As the caterpillar does this, its sleeping cells grow into future body parts. The process isn't immediate, but the cells do develop exponentially in a short period of time.

That protein-rich soup fuels the rapid cell division required to reach key markers that are the formation of wings, antennae, legs, eyes, genitals, and all the other features of an adult butterfly. Each of these markers along the way from cell generation to bodily parts are small wins. Each takes time and each needs to be worked on separately.

If you're leading any sort of transformation, I encourage you to spend two minutes watching a video titled "Temporal Study of Chrysalis Development," created by scientists associated with the University of Manchester.[40] It deftly illustrates the transformation process, which is complex, interdependent, and takes time—universal characteristics for almost all transformations.

I talk about the digital transformation having pit stops (or markers), and within each pit stop will be a range of mini-wins. There is a common misconception that the destination is the end of the transformation. It is not. It's about the journey. And the journey, like the cell formation in the

---

39   Ferris Jabr, "How Does a Caterpillar Turn into a Butterfly?" *Scientific American*, August 10, 2021, https://www.scientificamerican.com/article/caterpillar-butterfly-metamorphosis-explainer/.

40   Temporal Study of Chrysalis Development," Manchester X-Ray Imaging Facility, Engineering and Physical Sciences Research Council, and The University of Manchester, YouTube video, May 14, 2013, https://youtu.be/GxyZSzs7Seg.

butterfly, is made up of many small wins. It needs to be seen that way on a continuous basis.

For transformations to be successful, you will need small wins. Then you will need to iterate around these wins constantly because your goalposts will change with time. This mindset needs to be inculcated into the culture of any transformation program. Don't make the mistake of sitting still and celebrating coming out of the hyper-care period of a program. That doesn't mean you have transformed, only that you've gone live. Now you begin to shape the next iteration in transforming your organization.

The caterpillar and butterfly don't just look different. They are different. They behave differently. One lives in trees and is deemed a pest. The other flies and is admired for its beauty. One eats leaves. The other lives off nectar.

The same is true for your organization's digital transformation. After your transformation, your organization should strategize and operate much differently than it did before. If your digital transformation doesn't result in achieving the impact (business results) you sought in the first place, then you haven't actually undergone a digital transformation.

To measure impact, an organization must start off knowing what levers they are trying to shift. Do you know what levers you are trying to impact? Can you readily measure the impact? Are they tied to your operational and financial metrics? Are you able to measure the impact of your tech investments on these metrics? If not, what you have done is put in a lot of work, spent a bucket load of money, and gambled a significant amount of leadership credibility only to stop short of solving the day-in-the-life scenarios of your organization. This is typically the black hole faced by most organizations, and this is where DAPs come in.

It doesn't matter how many files you digitize. Or how many slick new enterprise-wide software applications you launch. It doesn't even matter how many people you train (because more than likely you're training was ineffective; more on that later).

If the impact isn't there, you haven't transformed. What you've done, to put it bluntly, is fail. Usually, quite expensively.

The reason for this is not a mystery, nor should it be. As we've seen time and time again, when a large organization looks to improve, it typically focuses on the paying customer. It's as if an organization views its customer as a special best friend deserving of its full attention. Meanwhile, its employees are almost second-class citizens. Whenever an investment is made in employee tools, that full attention to user satisfaction for employees is lacking or in some cases almost non-existent. Not only is this simple, but it's also selfish and short-sighted.

To truly improve, an organization needs to apply a little design thinking. First, put the user (your customers or your employees, depending on the situation) at the center of the desired outcome. Does your design factor in the ability to access all necessary applications so you can work from anywhere?

Next, reframe the problem from their perspective in the center. What does the user/customer/employee at the center need to achieve that overall desired outcome? This is the basis for disruption and, not coincidentally, also the basis for a truly successful digital transformation.

I have a simple test for companies and their senior executives: I ask them to show me how they use the underlying technologies in their digital transformations they've sanctioned to purchase.

Most times, they can't show me how they are investing their time in the journey. So, if they are not actively participating, how can they understand the problem at hand?

The Power of How

I have to admit that much of the inspiration for this book has come from my curious mind. As the youngest of three children, I was often left to my own devices, and many times I was confronted with obstacles that I needed to simply deal with. Whether it was how to fix the breaks on my bike or how to negotiate my way out of homework to spend more time at the park, my mind has always worked to find reasons and possibilities.

In April 2016, I embarked on a digital transformation journey myself.

Ours was the 25,000-employee, 13-country human resources system implementation I mentioned earlier. As we progressed through evaluations and demonstrations, it became evident that we were going to have a problem. Our business was manufacturing. How were we going to get factory workers—employees who were by and large uncomfortable or unfamiliar with digital technology—to care about (never mind use) new technology?

While this was a core consideration, my mind shifted to survival mode. Can we get through this unscathed? Will I lose my job? Will my boss lose his job? Will we blow out budgets? The panic set in. This is when I found DAP.

Because I've been there myself, I know the mindset of most executives, whether they're buying a new software package or undertaking an organization-wide digital transformation. Companies typically ask themselves two questions: *What* and *why?*

What are we buying? Usually, it's software.

Why are we buying this? To solve a problem.

"What" and "why." These have been the two most important questions that strategy owners or buyers of software have focused on: "*What* is the problem I am trying to solve?" and "*Why* am I trying to solve this problem?"

At first glance, these seem to be the right questions to ask. But the reality is that after several hundreds of millions (in some cases billions) of wasted dollars and days, weeks, months, and years collectively spent trying, most companies have yet to experience the promised value of their software. In fact, it's not uncommon that the more software a company buys, the bigger their problems get. It goes something like this:

"Okay, we bought this sales software to help our sales team make more money. First, we have to integrate it with our other systems....

Then we have to train our salespeople to use it....

Then we have to make sure our salespeople are actually using it."

And heaven forbid the software is updated with significant improvements. "Improvements" is another word for changes, and changes have the power to rouse frustration for those experiencing the changes.

One can argue that these are just problems to solve; the inherent tasks that come with the territory when buying and implementing new software. That's true. But they also happen to be the reason so many of these efforts—be it one piece of software or an attempt at a full-scale digital transformation—fall short of the desired outcome that initiated the software shopping spree in the first place.

Don't believe me? Here is a simple test. Walk up to a group of salespeople and ask them about their quarterly forecast. Heck, ask them about next quarter. See how many open their CRM system, or more unsurprisingly, how many open up their special Excel file. I'm guessing that's hardly what their executives had in mind when they approved the last round of expensive sale-support software and training.

Instead of asking "What can an application do?" or "Why did we buy the application?" they need to consider the subtle nuance in a simple, three-letter word: *how*. As in, "*How* do we use the application to realize the value from it that we desire?"

Because "*How?*" is the question at the heart of all successful digital transformations. *How* are we going to solve this problem? *How* are we going to implement this new software with the end *users* in mind? *How* will that affect other parts of our business?

Answer the question *How?* and, like the Australian insurance company, you'll be able to point your organization toward a rapid, true digital transformation, navigating any obstacle that may arise in your path.

And, trust me, they will arise. The Power of How is Now.

Things to Consider

I encourage you to think about one or two core corporate objectives that you may be accountable for in some shape or form. Do you know what success looks like? If you don't, then ask someone. Can they define and articulate what good looks like, never mind measure?

Ask yourself what you need to do to be able to impact those metrics. Keep asking yourself how do you impact or can you impact those metrics.

Chances are you will stumble upon two key challenges:

The complexity of your business processes ("Where do I find this thing?" "It took too long." "I got lost.").

The friction posed by your technology investments ("Hey, I don't know how to use this thing!").

This is where the world of DAP begins. This is where the Power of How will start to germinate within your thinking.

For extra credit, you may want to track down a financial analyst who can share with you the assumptions that were made in the original business case regarding the impact of technology on the return of investment calculation. Imagine being able to impact, de-risk, accelerate, and maximize the initial assumptions. Welcome to DAP.

CHAPTER 3

THE PROMISE OF DIGITAL TRANSFORMATION

Your success or failure will be determined by people being able to do the things you need them to do in your new world.

Standard Chartered is a global banking and financial services company based in London, whose name is the result of a 1969 merger of The Chartered Bank of India, Australia, and China and Standard Bank of British South Africa. With company origins more than 150 years old, it's an institution operating in 59 markets that span 125 nationalities.[41] With such a base of diverse customers and employees, it behooves Standard Chartered to be active and attentive to its internal culture.

Or as Standard Chartered's Group Head of HR Tanuj Kapilashrami put it on the podcast myHRfuture, "All of the work on culture is in service of improving our client service, client experience, and ultimately our performance."[42]

---

41 "About Us: We're Here for Good," Standard Chartered, accessed May 13, 2021, https://www.sc.com/en/about/.

42 David Green, interview with Tanuj Kapilashrami, "20: Designing an Exceptional Employee Experience," October 29, 2019, in myHRfuture, podcast, https://www.myhrfuture.com/digital-hr-leaders-podcast/2019/10/29/designing-an-exceptional-employee-experience.

Standard Chartered focuses its energy on employee experience, Kapilashrami says, because it's critical to align employee experience and work with the company's mission to deliver a tailored customer experience.

Otherwise, she says, "if you don't focus on experience, it's really a race to the bottom."[43]

As an example, she points to their HR processes. Rather than going through traditional channels—intranet sites, massive policy documents, or calling up people in HR—Standard Chartered implemented a DAP that she describes as "a very intuitive process" that guides employees through the basic HR processes.[44]

Part of the beauty of a DAP is in its simplicity. A process owner can simply log into a content curation tool (aka the editor) and begin to create content tailored to a specific process. This content, Kapilashrami said, includes small blurbs, question marks, and other on-screen signals to guide people through the process.

As one example of Standard Chartered's success using a DAP to transform its employees' experience, Kapilashrami pointed to the company's goal setting and review process. As with a lot of companies, Standard Chartered managers sit down with their direct reports to establish that person's goals for the year. Then midyear, the managers get together with their reports to review how the person is faring in meeting their goals.

Those midyear reviews take place over one month and that month is the only time managers can access the HR software to update the goals. After implementing their DAP, Kapilashrami says, 90 percent of Standard Chartered's managers used the performance review software. This is in comparison to the previous year when only 13 percent accessed their intranet to update the goal tracking application.[45]

Ahem, please read that again.

Standard Chartered went from 13 percent to *90 percent* of its employees using the company's goal tracking software! All because their new way

---

43   Ibid.

44   Ibid.

45   Ibid.

of working held the employee's hand through a journey across unfamiliar ground. People were proactively engaged, tactically guided and where it made logical sense, steps were automated to teleport the user successfully through to the finish line. All this with the use of the company's DAP. This digital concierge brought the process to life. It was like a breath of fresh air sweeping through a room.

Kapilashrami goes on to say they were also able to calculate that over a two-month window where everyone does their midyear reviews, about 60 percent of their people used a DAP quick-reference guide. It was a sort of digital concierge service on the screen explaining to people what things mean and what they needed to do at a particular place in the process. All the guidance was in real-time and on the fly.

The effects on productivity were astounding. Using a DAP saved each employee who used the system 40 minutes, Kapilashrami says.[46]

No surprise then that results like that had immediate internal implications. She says that very quickly conversations across all of Standard Chartered shifted from talking about the latest "sexy technology" to "How does that experience translate to greater productivity, giving people that time to have 40 minutes extra to have better quality conversations?"[47]

That is just one example of how a DAP can turn an obstacle to your success (people) into the key to your success (the same people) by rapidly nurturing their baby users into sophisticated users.

Perhaps this is an opportune moment to peel back the layers of the onion a little. Some of you may be asking yourself, "Why is this example such a big deal?" Please allow me the opportunity to explain.

Think about it: here is a process (midyear review) that (let's face it), a) nobody likes to do and, b) most people don't remember how to do it because they are called to do it once or twice a year, at most.

Now here is where the criticality comes into place. Let's view the goal-setting process through the company's rationale.

Companies don't buy HR software because it's fun. They buy it because

---

46   Ibid.
47   Ibid.

they're trying to bridge the gap between their business strategy and their business results. The strategic intent of HR and HR Tech has always been to help leaders bridge the execution gap between business strategy and corporate results. Yup, all those hours spent filling those digital goal forms at the start of the year actually have strategic significance.

The theory suggests that an execution gap exists because of an organization's inability to execute. The key to solving this is to better align the troops, ensuring they're deployed in the right places to remove as much friction from the execution as possible. The goal form is a mechanism to ensure that alignment exists between the troops and the outcome. Who would have thought that the mundane goal form and performance review process would yield so much power?

Now if you apply that to the Standard Chartered example, you can suddenly see why their results with a DAP on this simple process were so compelling. It's a clear-cut, if not a humble, example of software leading to better outcomes for a company and how a DAP can help the people who need to use the software actually use it.

Let's Get Agile

Another movement began to take shape in the early 2000s. Business leaders began to experience a significant lag in innovation cycles within their "innovation" teams. The world was changing more dramatically than ever. Businesses and entire industries were being disrupted at an alarming rate. Nobody (well almost nobody,) imagined Airbnb could disrupt the hotel chain industry so dramatically.

In December 2020, Airbnb had a market cap of $86.5 billion. To give you a sense, the market cap of both the Marriott and Hilton Hotel groups was $42 billion and $29 billion, respectively.[48]

It took a 32-year-old disruptor named Elon Musk to rethink the car industry. Traditional manufacturing aside, data was his fuel. As of Decem-

---

48   Lauren Feiner, "Airbnb Skyrockets 112% in Public Market Debut, Giving It a Market Cap of $86.5 Billion," CNBC, December 10, 2020, https://www.cnbc.com/2020/12/10/airbnb-ipo-abnb-starts-trading-on-the-nasdaq.html.

ber 2020, the market cap of Tesla is greater than that of the next nine largest automotive companies.[49] Some may argue that he is dishing out a better car, but the crux of his disruption was that he digitally transformed the automotive industry to be a data-based industry.[50] Given that strategy, it doesn't really matter what the competition does. With each additional Tesla vehicle on the road, Tesla generates data at a scale that acts as a competitive advantage.

These two examples made one thing crystal clear: the world was changing faster than traditional businesses or business mindsets (more on this later) could keep up.

Enter a "new" business paradigm: the agile framework. It shifted the mindset from the individual's task in the process to a team-based approach where a team comprised a range of skills and experiences. It seemed logical that this "scrum" approach of assembling teams with specialist skills akin to an NFL or NBA team made sense.

But a flaw began to appear as a result of this schoolyard picks method, one that can have a significant impact on an organization's ability to execute.

Once the teams have been picked, so to speak, there are some people who didn't get the nod to join a team. In many cases, these individuals are either reassigned to different parts of the organization or, worse yet, excused permanently.

Again, logically this seems to make sense. But this approach has a critical flaw in that it ignores the notion of collective tribal knowledge that exists within functions rather than individuals. By separating them, you haven't strengthened corporate muscle memory, but have actually weakened it. Imagine all that richness of experience walking out the door.

Yes, you've reduced business costs, maybe impacted your P&L, and even got a positive bump in the short-term share price, which may have bought you an additional six months in the hot seat. But in doing so, you've also

---

49 Michael Wayland and Lora Kolodny, "Tesla's Market Cap Tops the 9 Largest Automakers Combined—Experts Disagree About if That Can Last," CNBC, December 14, 2020, https://www.cnbc.com/2020/12/14/tesla-valuation-more-than-nine-largest-carmakers-combined-why.html.

50 Ophelia Research, "Tesla Is a Data Company at Worst," Seeking Alpha, November 3, 2020, https://seekingalpha.com/article/4384318-tesla-is-data-company-worst.

let a bucket load of tribal knowledge walk out the door. And there was plenty of benefit to having all this tribal knowledge together.

Now pause and ask yourself if you ever needed to do a critical business process in a system only to be told that only, say, Marge knew how to get it done? But Marge is no longer in the building because, well, she didn't get picked.

What do you do now? That's when DAP suddenly comes alive.

Before all that tribal knowledge went out the door, you could have re-thought how you could have best leveraged Marge's experience. Maybe she could have been part of the team that built out all the content on your DAP, forever cementing that tribal process knowledge that had served the organization for so long.

Opportunity, Challenge, or Mistake?

If you look at software spending by companies, the annual global software spend to solve digital transformation problems has become more than $600 billion a year.[51] And that's just the software side. Of course, you want to get the most value out of all the software you bought so throw services into the mix at a ratio of 5:1 and we're looking at spending in the neighborhood of $3 trillion on digital transformation. That's more than the GDP of France in 2019.[52]

But let's be clear, how companies pursue that digital transformation can turn out to be a $3 trillion opportunity, challenge, or mistake.

In 2019, the Everest group reported that 78 percent of digital transformations failed to meet their business objectives.[53] Put in another way, only a meager 22 percent of projects were deemed successful. Whilst I am not a gambling man, it appears you have more chance of winning at a game of calling heads-or-tails with a toss of a coin than realizing, never mind

---

51 Agrawal and Bartlett, "Software 2019: IPOS, M&A, and Forces of Growth—Here's Software 2019."

52 "France GDP," Trading Economics, accessed May 19, 2021, https://tradingeconomics.com/france/gdp.

53 Jimit Arora, "Digital Transformation Success Is NOT Rooted in Technology | Blog," Everest Group, September 11, 2019, https://www.everestgrp.com/2019-09-digital-transformation-success-is-not-rooted-in-technology-blog-51242.html.

reaping, the benefits of the transformation.

Okay, that's on what and how much companies are spending. But why are they spending all this money on software?

Because they're looking to create efficiencies that significantly drive their profit and loss. They are trying to improve that P&L through customer interactions and employee productivity. More specifically, they're looking to leverage five areas that cut across all industries:

1. Drive self-service.

2. Improve data quality.

3. Reduce support costs.

4. Improve compliance processes.

5. Spur continuous process improvement.

Companies want to reduce the cost of serving customers without reducing quality. A big part of reducing support costs is driving self-service for customers so companies can staff support centers with fewer people and hire more revenue-generating assets. There is some genuine intent around this. Call centers have notoriously high turnover rates, and it takes significant time to get new employees up to speed. If I can get the customer to self-serve, not only do we reduce call volume, we also avoid an increase in average handling times. That means we reduce our cost to serve. And if I can get the new call center agent productive quicker and able to handle multiple process queries competently, then I know I have unearthed a positive multiplier effect.

And, lastly, they're banking that all of this together will lead to ongoing analysis that allows the organization to constantly assess and improve processes and functions. But do not miss the endgame—all these efforts must result in positive outcomes for a company's profit and loss sheet.

Here's an example from my own experience.

Once, at a previous job, I was using a piece of HR software to complete performance reviews. For as long as I had used this application, the button to complete and submit the review was always displayed at the bottom right of the screen. But one day I went into the application to complete my direct reports' performance reviews only to find the button was not where it had always been.

That mild panic we all feel when things change without warning washed over me. "The button is NOT at the bottom right?!"

Facing this updated version of the software, I was in essence a baby user with the application all over again.

So, what's the first thing I did? I phoned a friend. As if I was on that game show *Who Wants to Be a Millionaire?* but with higher stakes. Well, to me at that moment anyway. And to my direct reports too.

My friend was more than simply a friend. He was, in fact, my human resources business partner. After I explained my situation, he calmly told me that they'd conducted a session on the changes two weeks prior. They had even sent out the Webex recording, a video, and a bunch of instructional guides.

"You obviously didn't pay attention," he said, "I can't show you where it is right now because I am out to lunch."

Some friend. After that, I went around asking my colleagues if they knew anything about the missing button. You know, polling the audience. But that was also to no avail.

Their responses ranged from "Why are you bothering me with this right now? I'm busy," to "Raj, I really haven't even thought about it. Good luck finding your button."

The Button Has Now Become a Thing

Now imagine this Missing Button Thing was a company-wide issue or a product-wide issue caused by a software update. What if all the other baby users sharing my missing button anxiety were to call a support center rather than, say, bother their friends and coworkers?

It would put a significant strain on the center in terms of increased call volumes, longer hold times, longer service times, and so on, leading to additional costs related to adding staff to successfully handle the increased volume.

Let's look at the Missing Button predicament from the support center perspective. For the sake of argument, let's say a support center gets 1,000 calls a month. Over a year, that's 12,000 calls (1,000 calls x 12 months).

Now let's say those calls take 30 minutes to resolve. And let's assume a call center agent gets paid $20 an hour.

Now, this Missing Button Thing is generating more calls to the call center. Increasing call volume causes average handling time to go up an extra 15 minutes, to 45 minutes from 30 minutes because maybe, due to your attrition rates, you've got a new bunch of baby user agents working the phones.

Now we have to multiply those 12,000 calls annually by an extra 15 minutes per call. That's 180,000 minutes. Divide that 180,000 by 60 (60 minutes in an hour) and we get 3,000 more hours.

Okay, now multiply that 3,000 hours by the $20-an-hour a call center agent gets paid. That's an additional cost of $60,000 per year. And remember, that's just one issue. You can see how the costs add up quickly.

Now imagine the support staff can help employees or customers to help themselves—service calls—then the company doesn't have to staff up to handle all those "What happened to the button?" calls.

Even if the company turns just 20 to 30 percent of those calls into self-service calls, the results can be significant.

In a call center, the biggest metric is managing the average call time or average handling time as it is commonly known. Let's say a call center has an average handling time of 30 minutes for a specific process and there is a fixed number of agents.

Now let's cue the next problem with agent attrition. The stark reality is that a baby agent simply doesn't have the experience to deal with these calls in an efficient manner. He or she needs time to mature, to learn to crawl, walk before running.

Again, if a call takes too long, it means an additional increase in average handling times because other customers are waiting on hold for longer periods before they even connect with call center staff.

On top of that, the new hires have less experience, of course, so they have to train them. Now there are related training costs involved too. Even with training, it will take time for the new support hires to gain the experience to deal with even the most routine issues. In other words, average call handling times go up.

So that's one layer of around cost and compensation. Then there's the second layer: friction.

The person who should care about all this is the executive sitting comfortably in his or her corner office instead of living and experiencing the frustrations of the team on the ground. This executive should care because he or she is the one who has to go back and tell the shareholders that support cost infrastructure went through the roof while the company got a less positive outcome with customers. All because a software upgrade did something with a button.

An alternative might be that the executive goes back to the shareholders and explains what the challenges were and how the company has resolved the challenges by rethinking how they work so that even the most inexperienced baby users can now execute on the role.

But what if a call center can deflect those types of common support questions? The impact in the business is potentially huge on just this one support question alone.

The company might employ a DAP to help customers help themselves (self-serve) online. Rather than having a customer support representative spend time solving this very common problem, the customer is guided by a DAP toward finding the solution to their very common question. The person gets through their call problem and accurately.

It also deflects the volume of calls requiring assistance from a rep, freeing the rep to deal with other more intricate or rare calls. There is no need to hire additional staff, meaning no new costs related to new hires and training.

Also, while the customer is self-servicing, the company can validate the data at the point where it's being entered, thus lowering errors and improving the quality of the data.

This information can be used to then refine the process further or applied to other processes as needed. Plus, there's an added benefit of being able to use analytics to identify what's going well for the employee and what they need help with.

When multiplied across the support center, all this improves the center's capacity to handle more calls, shortening average call handling times, and getting cleaner, more accurate data. Customers are happier because the support centers get them through the support process faster. This reduces the average handling times but, on the flipside, also increases customer satisfaction and loyalty. This very well may protect revenue, but will engender trust leading to more advocacy and profits.

By default, that impacts the cost to serve. Which in turn impacts the company's profit and loss. That's quite a lot to get from just one process optimization. And that's the very real promise of digital transformation.

Once you understand the true impact of digital transformation, you can see why companies have spent so much money (again, over $3 trillion in software and service) in pursuit of it.

But any attempt at transformation can easily turn into stagnation with unhappy employees, unhappy customers, and an unhappy business. Ironically, the things companies pursue to thrive ultimately may result in their extinction because they don't focus on *how*. They must ask themselves, how do the software, services, and training we're investing in affect the people who use it? How are we impacting humanity one software application at a time?

People are at the center of all this technology and how well they take advantage of all the technology and training is the key to how successful a digital transformation will be.

Case in point, I eventually found the missing button. The interface designers had relocated it to the upper left corner.

But you can see how neglecting to put the baby user at the center of even a slight change in the interface of a familiar piece of software can have significant ramifications in terms of time, resources and money.

And yet, unlike Standard Chartered, a shocking majority of organizations do neglect their baby users. And, as you'll see, much to their own detriment.

Do you have visibility as to where your digital transformation stands in the eyes of your users? While self-service strategies are not new, how are you measuring how much self-service you are driving through the organization? Do you have a sense of how many of your support tickets are similar in nature?

What would the cashable benefit of deflecting these be to your organization? What would the impact be to your operational metrics if you could deflect and have users complete 20 percent of tasks that they struggle with today?

More importantly, have you considered the impact of reducing average handling times for your customers? In the case of some Australian families, this was lifesaving.

CHAPTER 4

FAILURE ISN'T AN OPTION. IT'S PRACTICALLY A CERTAINTY

S orry to be the one to have to tell you this but your digital transformation is going to fail.

Please know that I'm not trying to be the messenger of doom and gloom predicting that your company's time, money, and efforts are all in vain. The numbers paint a stark picture:

- 84 percent of companies fail at digital transformation—*Forbes*[54]

- 50 percent of organizations will fail to achieve expected outcomes—*The Gartner Group*[55]

- Only eight percent of executives believe they have achieved digi-

---

54   Bruce Rogers, "Why 84% Of Companies Fail at Digital Transformation," *Forbes*, January 7, 2016, https://www.forbes.com/sites/brucerogers/2016/01/07/why-84-of-companies-fail-at-digital-transformation/?sh=2077c 35397bd.

55   "Gartner Predicts by 2021, CIOs Will Be as Responsible for Culture Change as Chief HR Officers," Gartner, February 11, 2019, https://www.gartner.com/en/newsroom/press-releases/2019-02-11-gartner-predicts-by-2021--cios-will-be-as-responsible.

tal transformation—*Ovum*[56]

While past performance hardly guarantees future results, as the saying goes, those who've gone before do not offer you much hope if you're looking to avoid pain. Fortunately, we have the cure. We know why the majority of digital transformations are sunk before they've even set sail.

The notion of digital transformations is great, right? I mean, who doesn't want to improve their customers' experience and improve employee productivity? So, companies went out and bought a bucket load of software—$600 billion worth[57]—in hopes of seeing at least a bump in productivity that would translate into a better customer experience.

But when you look at the stats, productivity has flattened out over that same period. Turns out, there hasn't been a strong material correlation between software spend and improvements in productivity which appears to have plateaued in the last 20-plus years.

And why was that? It's not about software in isolation. It's *how* (there is that pesky three-letter word again) people are using the software in the context of their business that really gets companies where they want to be. The only way for that to happen: If somehow software and humans got a bit friendlier with each other.

That's where the notion of a DAP was born. Remove the friction between software and the baby users by making software more human-like, then organizations will see that increase in efficiency, productivity, and experience because users will start to crawl, walk, and run faster. It all begins by putting the user at the heart of the journey.

So, the good news is a DAP can help you to overcome the challenges of transforming your company. But first we need to understand why the success rates are so abysmal.

---

[56] John Moore, "Digital Transformation: Services Firms May Find Work Across Verticals," SearchITChannel, December 1, 2017, https://searchitchannel.techtarget.com/news/450431196/Digital-transformation-Services-firms-may-find-work-across-verticals.

[57] Agrawal and Bartlett, "Software 2019: IPOs, M&A, and Forces of Growth—Here's Software 2019."

The Roots of Failure

First and foremost, most organizations don't really understand the definition of success. Ask an executive how they will measure their success and they'll likely give you the easy answer that it's about improving profit and loss. What happened to being a butterfly?

That's not success. That's an outcome of a successful transformation and, obviously, a highly desirable one.

But the devil is in the details. To get into the details, we need to take more responsibility in being able to link technical dependency goals to operational metrics that flow into the P&L as materialized cash benefits. This may sound like technical speak but simply put, think of it like the domino effect. If one domino is out of sync then the rest will not get triggered.

Here's a simple definition of a successful digital transformation: *People adopting digital tools to do their job better in the service of desired business outcomes.*

When you really boil it down, success is the impact your efforts have. Now, "better" can mean more efficiently, accurately, rapidly, or, ideally, all three. Sometimes "better" means simply *getting* people to use the new tools you've invested in.

Less obvious though is the word "adoption." When I ask people what "adoption" means, I've found it's quite a confrontational question, mainly because everybody thinks, "Oh, it's easy. I know the answer."

Humor me before reading on. Please grab a scrap of paper and try to write down your definition of adoption. Now have a go at defining what digital adoption means to you. Not so easy, right?

Do we actually understand what the word "adopt" actually means? I thought it was an easy one for me too. After all, I do this for a living. Then I went to the dictionary and discovered something profound in the definition of adoption, something I hadn't considered before.

According to Merriam-Webster, to adopt something is to take up and practice or use something.[58] What is missing from that definition in my

---

58   Merriam-Webster, "adopt," accessed May 24, 2021, https://www.merriam-webster.com/dictionary/adopt#other-words.

opinion was the outcome of the "practice or use." For true adoption to take place, I believe *the action of using or doing something repeatedly must be done in a consistent manner and result in a positive (intended) outcome.* In the case of digital transformation, it means the repeated practice of using the new digital tools.

It's these four words, "in a consistent manner," that seem most critical to me. In a consistent manner comes down to the human psyche in itself, making it the primary challenge around getting people to use something new.

The first thing to remember is that human beings are just that—human beings. We're not robots. And as baby users, we all have a learning curve. It takes time for us to learn how to crawl, walk, and run. For us to learn things it takes repetition. Most of us understand the link between a learning curve and adoption, so much so that in his book *Outliers*, author Malcolm Gladwell popularized the 10,000 Hours Rule, as in it takes 10,000 hours of repeated practice to master something.[59]

But few people pay enough attention to our forgetting curve. This isn't a new phenomenon. As far back as 1885, the psychologist Hermann Ebbinghaus first hypothesized about the forgetting curve.[60]

He describes the forgetting curve as a decrease in the brain's ability to retain memory over time. He found that the rate of forgetting was impacted by factors such as the way information was presented and psychological elements such as increased stress and lack of sleep.

What's more, cognitive science researcher Art Kohn found that humans forget approximately 50 percent of new information *within the hour* in which they are presented with it! We go on to forget an average of 70 percent of new information within 24 hours. Kohn cites that the decay rate after a week is close to 90 percent.[61]

Simply put, our ability to retain, internalize, and cement new knowl-

---

59   Malcom Gladwell, *Outliers: The Story of Success* (New York: Back Bay Books, 2011).

60   Hermann Ebbinghaus, *Über das Gedächtnis* (Berlin: Duncker & Humblot, 1885).

61   Art Kohn, "Brain Science: The Forgetting Curve–the Dirty Secret of Corporate Training," Learning Solutions, March 13, 2014, https://learningsolutionsmag.com/articles/1379/brain-science-the-forgetting-curvethe-dirty-secret-of-corporate-training.

edge is pretty limited.

In the "old" software world, we used to get away with this. Back then, when we deployed a system, we could have training courses every six months or every year. Once we deployed a piece of software, changes would be few and far between. This afforded us the luxury of time to reach a certain level of proficiency and mastery with our "digital" tools. Add to that we had the benefit of an army of business partners ready to sit and hold our hand through the changes.

Because it wasn't unusual to have any changes with the software for two years or more, nobody really paid attention to the forgetting curve. It wasn't that big of a deal. Besides, there was plenty of time to relearn the software or have Marge come show us how to use it before an updated version came along. All the company needed to do was offer some additional training to get you back on the learning curve (which you probably would forget within 24 hours, according to Art Kohn). If you did remember, great. If not, don't worry, there would probably be a refresher down the road at the end of the year or at the start of the new one.

But along came two important technical advances, both of which failed to take into account the human element they were ultimately supposed to serve.

Lost in the Cloud

We now live in a cloud-first world driven by agile software development. This means incredible advancements in software happen very quickly. But unfortunately, many companies are stuck in what I call cloud 1.0.

They started their cloud transformation journey probably 10 to 15 years ago thinking of the cloud as a cheaper delivery model. They ran—in some cases sprinted—to the cloud to get rid of servers and free up perceived related costs. But they did this without an appreciation for the costs associated with learning to crawl, walk, and run with the new digital tools. They no longer had to dedicate real estate to housing servers or pay people to update the software, but unintended consequences arose.

That original premise for using the cloud was quite simple. Organizations had an opportunity to rethink their business processes, taking the opportunity to simplify how work got done. Here was an opportunity to reduce the burden of accommodating the more than a thousand ways to apply for time off. That number is not made up.

Just think about it, here we have an opportunity to not only simplify the system support costs due to the exotic number of permutations but also reduce the risk of not having Marge close by to explain how to execute on each of the 1,256 ways.

All that many of the first-generation organizations did was take their software and stick it in the cloud. They were not brave enough to tackle the beast of complexity that came with this new cloud world, which meant that all they got was an expensive, old process. My mentor best described it as putting lipstick on a pig (said in the broadest French accent.)

Or thinking of it another way, it's akin to taking an old 1963 car engine and trying to force it under the hood of a Tesla.

What companies should have done instead was take the opportunity to simplify, standardize, and take advantage of everything else the cloud allows them to do. Perhaps their biggest mistake as they seek digital transformation has been their failure to wrap a human element around the deployment element.

The next real challenge that the cloud brought to the fore was this notion of functional releases. To the less innovative organizations, there is a huge attraction to Software-as-a-Service (SaaS) applications because you are gaining access to the smarts, scars, and insights of an aggregated experience pool. You may be a midsized grocery chain, but you now have the benefit of what Walmart deems as innovation.

The software companies say, "Oh, look, all this new innovation! You can now use innovation as a competitive differentiator!" But no sooner have you read the email than they have said, "We're updating the system!"

The pace of changes is so rapid that if you wait six months or a year to train somebody, critical elements of the application have likely changed two or three times.

And each time there is an update or a new release, we as users have to start over to some degree or another. We retreat from running to walking and in many cases all the way back to crawling. It doesn't matter whether it's a software tweak or a full-on upgrade with a redesigned interface, it contributes to frustration with the baby user. Remember the missing/moved button in Chapter 2? It became a real "thing." And that means a loss of efficiency and productivity from employees simply because something changes.

For a specific example, let's think about it in terms of our call center agent from earlier. The agent has worked there for three years and has their digital tools down pat. When somebody changes something in the software that causes our agent to have to learn to use a new piece of functionality. This adds friction. Friction may impact average handling times (AHT), which in turn may have an impact on the P&L.

Now consider that the software the agent is using is cloud-based and changes are coming randomly and rapidly. This new rapid update/release cycle compounds the implications of any change for baby users, even one as simple as "where did the button go?"

Despite the fact we're now all living in a new cloud world, companies have yet to rethink their adoption strategies. We need to rethink this and quickly. We cannot continue to use 20th century mindsets to solve a 21st century conundrum. To continue will simply add more jet fuel to the already raging fire.

It's like turning up to a Formula One race with a car made in 1963. It doesn't have the same aerodynamics, efficiency, or speed. It lacks a competitive pit crew. Imagine if you turned around and your pit crew is taking two and a half minutes to change tires when your competitors are doing in 15 seconds? It's just not going to cut it. This then exposes senior leaders in their ability to execute their strategies.

Instead of reverting to the comfort of a technical implementation, companies should have approached upgrades and transformations using a day-in-the-life-of-a-user journey, so they could understand what their baby users needed.

Here's a simple, non-technical version of what I mean by a user journey. Let's say you want to visit your mum. Your journey will entail different pit stops. First, you need to pack your weekend bag. Then you remember to take the trash out, so the apartment doesn't smell while you are away. You then jump in the car and head to the freeway.

So far, so good. But then you realize you don't have enough gas to get you there so you look for the nearest gas station to fill up. All done, you remember that your mum asked you to stop off at the grocery store to pick up some eggs and milk for her. You remember Mum loves tulips, so your next stop has to be the florist.

As you leave the florist, you get a WhatsApp message from Mum asking you if you could do her a favor and pick up Max the dog from the neighbors before coming to her house. So, in your user journey from home to Mum's, you have had multiple, very different stops.

Each stop in this case represents different steps of a business process and potentially navigating through different software applications. Work doesn't typically happen in a single application. Some research suggests that the typical employee interacts with four or more digital touch points (applications) in a day. Typically, their path through processes isn't linear but rather meanders and branches off. Four digital touchpoints may not seem much, but what if I told you many Fortune 500 companies have in excess of 2,000 applications.[62] The scale of the challenge suddenly comes alive. Not knowing how to navigate the labyrinth is the real friction.

Worse still would be to find our baby users fearful and lost in the dark.

How big of an opportunity is this? Well, on average Fortune 500 companies spend in excess of $17,500 per user for end user computing, according to Dion Hinchcliffe, vice president and principal analyst of Constellation Research, a technology research firm.[63]

In the traditional software world, people are thinking about each one of the stops as a discreet segment unto itself rather than the interconnectivity of all those stops in a user journey. Imagine if I couldn't find the gas station

---

62 WalkMe. "CIO Perspective: Dion Hinchcliffe | Constellation Research," YouTube video, March 29, 2021, https://www.youtube.com/watch?v=xV_Klrohu5c.

63 Ibid.

or the grocery store or the florist. Imagine if I forgot to get Max!

However, if you did think about it as a journey rather than individual stops, you may have made different decisions around the technical implementation. Rather than looking at each stop on its own, your True North would certainly be different. The True North isn't going to the grocery store. It's not the florist. The True North is getting to Mum's house, navigating across state lines through seven or eight diverse pit stops.

The same is true when you start thinking about a digital transformation. Is your True North improving the output from a piece of software? Or is it to improve the output of people executing on your end-to-end digital processes to the benefit of your organization?

Now let's apply this user journey thinking to the day in the life of a salesperson. Yes, if you just fix how your CRM is used, perhaps you'll get a nice little bump upward in that application. But are you really transforming the end-to-end sales process?

The salesperson's end goal is to exceed their quota. To do that, the salesperson needs to interact with a whole bunch of software, much like you had to make several stops along the way in your journey to visit your mom.

For territory planning, a salesperson will probably have to use software like Outreach or Sales Navigator. Then once they finally have a conversation with a client, they need to go into a CRM to enter information about the opportunity.

Then they might need to turn to a different application to build out a price book. After that, they may need to turn to a different application for forecasting.

Once they know the deal's coming through, they might need to leverage a knowledge base around discounting policy. Then they may need to generate an order form.

Finally, they may need to figure out how to book that order.

When you think about that end-to-end journey, you see that the real power of transformation isn't about the point solution of improving how software is used. It's about reimagining the overall end-to-end process touching on each of those stops along the way. Think about the pressure of not knowing how to book an order as you struggle through that process at the eleventh-hour of the last day of the financial year.

But companies haven't been looking at all these sorts of interdependencies. Or the correlations between the two of the various stops, if you will. Companies need to change their mindset around how they approach the scale and the velocity of these changes. And the only way to do that is by using a digital adoption platform.

A DAP is that changing mindset. A DAP is that paradigm shift between the way of doing it in the past and the way they need to do it in the future (today).

Another aspect we need to embrace is the notion of digital IQ. Yup, this too is a thing. People shouldn't trivialize the significance of digital IQ or digital dexterity on digital tools. How we use technology varies so greatly among the full range of demographics, genders, cultures, and etcetera.

For instance, if you ask my mother-in-law if she uses digital technology, she'll say yes because she uses Facebook and email. But if, say, you go ask my friend's mother in the Philippines, she'll say yes because everything she does is on mobile digital apps.

Different people have different levels of competence around these things. This leads to another friction point when it comes up against the old way of building one set of training, a one-size-fits-all model. Today, given the differences in digital IQ and generations, people are looking for a far more curated experience that suits their specific needs.

The one-size-fits-all model doesn't work. The traditional isn't very good for building training programs customized for those different digital IQs and demographics. You essentially have to build the same program but customized for millennials, for Generation Y, for Generation X, Generation Z, for baby boomers, etc. Now all you're doing is creating a mess of varying training models that are a nightmare to keep up to date for all your audiences. Where do you as an organization sit on the Digital Aptitude spectrum? (See Figure 2.)

How would you characterize the digital aptitude of the employees throughout your organization?

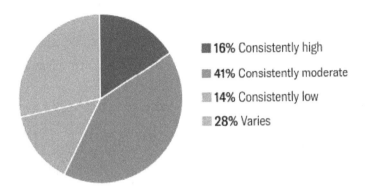

■ **16%** Consistently high

■ **41%** Consistently moderate

■ **14%** Consistently low

■ **28%** Varies

Figure 2: Digital Aptitude: So-So at Best: Most Companies Rate the Digital Aptitude of Their People as Middling or Mixed [64]

Instead, companies need a nimbler strategy to keep their people relevant and executing their jobs daily. They need to pay attention to learning curves and forgetting curves if they want their employees to use digital tools proficiently and consistently.

Often people generalize that digital IQ is a generational challenge. But it's naive to assume that older generations have a lower digital IQ than younger generations. Digital IQs are based on a range of factors including culture, demographics, and exposure and access to technology. All you have to do is look to the Philippines to realize that is not the case. In January 2021, over 70 percent of internet users aged between 55 and 65 years of age were active on e-commerce sites in the Philippines. In Thailand, over 72 percent of internet users aged between 55 and 65 years of age purchased a product online.[65]

The developing nations have used technology as a leapfrog strategy. This has helped to prime the older generation in the nations to lead from the forefront when it comes to all things digital. In fact, among these users,

---

64   Source: Harvard Business Review Analytic Services Survey, December 2020.

65   Simon Kemp, "Digital 2021: Thailand," DataReportal, February 11, 2021, https://datareportal.com/reports/digital-2021-thailand.

there is a general belief that if there isn't a mobile application for the task then it mustn't be worth doing. Now given that digital has become a core part of their everyday lives, any changes in their digital lives cannot come across as being pronounced or drastic.

Over 13 years ago in 2007, the Vodafone Group launched M-Pesa, a mobile phone-based money transfer, payments, and micro financing service to serve the "unbanked" in Kenya.[66] The M stands for mobile and Pesa translates into money in Swahili.[67] A decade after its launch, M-Pesa's transfers now account for almost half of Kenya's GDP.[68]

From a consumer experience perspective, enterprises realize these experiences are critical to their survival. They focus their time and energy here applying science, tech muscle, and investment to the consumer experience with a singular goal of removing the friction between the service provider and the consumer. You see in the consumer world where the consumer demands attention and controls the narrative, and so is heard loud and clear.

For instance, research has shown that cart abandonment rates on e-commerce sites can be as high as 70 percent, meaning billions of dollars of potential lost revenue.[69] That is why Amazon's patented 1-Click to cart functionality was such a game-changer to the industry. It simplified the world of the overwhelmed consumer. Just one click and you are done. While there are no confirmed details of the value 1-Click brought to Amazon, one estimate suggests that the patent impacted sales by as much as five percent, valuing the patent at $2.4 billion annually.[70]

There are many examples of companies' management failing to do these things at the outset only to have their digital transformation fail miserably. In turn, this has had an impact on the tenures of executives who do not get to experience the fruit of the transformation strategies.

---

66   "M-Pesa," Vodafone, accessed May 14, 2021, https://www.vodafone.com/what-we-do/services/m-pesa.

67   Julia Kagan, "M-Pesa," Investopedia, updated October 31, 2020, https://www.investopedia.com/terms/m/mpesa.asp.

68   Thomas McGrath, "M-PESA: How Kenya Revolutionized Mobile Payments," *N26 Magazine*, April 9, 2018, https://mag.n26.com/m-pesa-how-kenya-revolutionized-mobile-payments-56786bc09ef.

69   Emil Kristensen, "15 Cart Abandonment Statistics You Must Know in 2021," Sleeknote, March 11, 2021, https://sleeknote.com/blog/cart-abandonment-statistics.

70   Mike Arsenault, "How Valuable is Amazon's 1-Click Patent? It's Worth Billions," Rejoiner, accessed May 14, 2021, https://rejoiner.com/resources/amazon-1clickpatent/.

One example in particular shows both the downside of not thinking about the end-to-end process journey and the upside of thinking beyond quarterly shareholder returns.

Under Armour's Underperformance

In early October 2017, Patrik Frisk, then president and chief operating officer of Under Armour, had an incredibly important analyst meeting where he would need to present the company results for the previous quarter.[71] Under Armour had been the darling of the sports apparel world, and some experts suggested that they were leading the pack when it came to redefining the science of sporting goods.

Under Armour had bet the house on the digital transformation of their enterprise software planning technology stack, or ERP for short. The alarming news was that they had missed their numbers and there were bigger bumps ahead. The call was going to be uncomfortable for everyone involved, but it was the type of call that could have been career limiting.

There were a few factors to Under Armour's poor results—earnings were down significantly from the previous year—but there was no denying that chief among them was the poor execution of the core digital transformation program. The facts laid out between Frisk and David Bergman, the company's CFO, were as follows:

> ...we have implemented systems upgrades, including the July 1 launch of our integrated ERP business solution. And while these enhancements are designed to enable us to more effectively and efficiently operate our business and, ultimately, enhance productivity for the long term, the implementation caused disruption in our supply chain operations during the quarter. This led to delayed shipments and loss of productivity, which negatively impacted our third quarter results.

---

71   Angus Loten and Sara Germano, "Under Armour Links Sales Decline to Software Upgrade," the *Wall Street Journal*, October 31, 2017, https://www.wsj.com/articles/under-armour-links-sales-decline-to-software-upgrade-1509500544?tesla=y.

During this system migration, we have encountered a number of change management issues impacting our workforce and manufacturing partners as they adapt to the new platform and processes.[72]

As Frisk and Bergman dived into the root causes it became extremely clear that "the change management effort had been underestimated not merely from an internal stakeholder perspective but with inventory partners and other vendors."[73] They had missed the end-to-end user journey in the planning and underestimated the magnitude of the effort to get everyone crawling, walking, and running in their new world.

The impact was the announcement that earnings would need to be revised down in 2017 from $0.37 a share to between $0.18 to $0.20 a share.[74] Wall Street was not pleased and reacted accordingly. Under Armour stock fell from a high of $30.47 in January 2017 to a low of $11.61 on November 3, 2017.[75]

It would not have been unusual if that had been Frisk's last quarterly earnings call, but the company demonstrated great foresight and trust to stick by Frisk and Berman.

This commitment to business principles beyond quarterly earnings has since provided long-term dividends, both financially and in terms of satisfaction among employees, vendors, and customers. It allows executives to get into the guts of these transformations and course correct.

As for Frisk, as of this writing, he is now president and CEO of Under Armour, thanks in part to his ability to lead the company as it corrected its course to get its digital transformation on track.

Other companies have not been so patient. They've failed to recognize that the costs of ignoring a baby user's path to mastery and being unclear on the definition of a successful transformation program are enormous.

---

72 Larry Dignan, "Under Armour cites change management woes with SAP implementation as digital transformation stumbles," ZDNet, November 1, 2017, https://www.zdnet.com/article/under-armour-cites-change-management-woes-with-sap-implementation-as-digital-transformation-stumbles/.

73 Ibid.

74 Ibid.

75 "Under Armour Inc Class A," Google Finance, accessed May 24, 2021, https://www.google.com/finance/quote/UAA:NYSE?sa=X&ved=2ahUKEwijj6K54tnwAhUUIbcAHXNaDoIQ_AUoAXoECAEQAw&window=MAX.

The focus needs to be on the people who use the technology and where they are failing and why they are overwhelmed.

In 2015, General Electric launched a new business called GE Digital to help break into the digital space.[76] The goal was to harness the vast amounts of data within the GE family and become a digital powerhouse. They poured billions of dollars into the endeavor but soon lost focus on its initial mission.[77] They started to focus on short-term goals rather than standing true to the original mission of innovations. Not only did they waste those billions, but the CEO was forced to step aside. Nike halved its initial digital unit, Procter and Gamble wanted to be the most "digital company on the planet" but they too ran into difficulties with the mission.

I think Thomas Davenport and George Westerman summed it up best in their HBR article, "Why So Many High-Profile Digital Transformations Fail."

Digital is not just a thing that you can buy and plug into the organization.

Digital transformation is an ongoing process of changing the way you do business. It requires mixing people, machines, and business processes, with all of the messiness that entails. It also requires continuous monitoring and intervention, from the top.[78]

I believe Dion Hinchcliffe put it best in his research where he simply said, "Adoption is not automatic."[79]

Have you thought about these elements? Are some, most if not all these baked into your transformation strategy? If you have ticked some of these boxes, then you are ready to elevate your transformation program to include a digital adoption strategy.

---

76   "Creation of GE Digital," General Electric, September 14, 2015, https://www.ge.com/news/press-releases/creation-ge-digital.

77   Keith Kitani, "The $900 Billion Reason GE, Ford, and P&G Failed at Digital Transformation," CNBC, October 30, 2019, https://www.cnbc.com/2019/10/30/heres-why-ge-fords-digital-transformation-programs-failed-last-year.html.

78   Thomas H. Davenport and George Westerman, "Why So Many High-Profile Digital Transformations Fail," *Harvard Business Review*, March 9, 2018, https://hbr.org/2018/03/why-so-many-high-profile-digital-transformations-fail.

79   "Digital Adoption Is Not Automatic | Webinar Preview with Dion Hinchcliffe," YouTube video, March 26, 2021, https://www.youtube.com/watch?v=XtTM_EXM23k.

CHAPTER 5

MEET THE OVERWHELMED EMPLOYEE

M ost organizations don't realize they are home to a group of employees who simply cannot handle the additional expectations of digital
transformation programs. Meet the overwhelmed employee.

Now I don't need a bunch of research to tell me that this is a thing
because I have firsthand knowledge; I am an overwhelmed employee (at
times). But the research does make for compelling reading.

Organizations need to realize that the overwhelmed employee takes
many different shapes and forms and should never be confused for a low
digital IQ user. Imagine if we put the same amount of effort, smarts, and
muscle into the overwhelmed employee as we do to the overwhelmed consumer? Imagine the value we could realize; imagine how we could leverage
that as a talent acquisition differentiator. Imagine if we could avoid the
first-day churn of new hires?

The corporate workday week has changed quite dramatically in part
due to the proliferation of technology, in part due to silent expectations
of employers, and, in part, the fear of the employee that they may not be

doing enough.

Many people are working more than 60 hours a week. The boundaries of their professional and personal lives are undeniably merging. Mobility solutions haven't helped either. We are all connected 24/7, fidgeting with our phones 150 times a day, trying to figure out what's coming in—whether it's a text message, a WhatsApp message, an email, or something else.

Amid this new way of working, your company is flooding you with new things to learn because the organization is going through something called a digital transformation. You are confronted with a bunch of new things to learn because they've shifted from old software to new software applications.

Oh, and by the way, that new software? It's just been updated. That damn button just moved again!

I don't need to see you to know that many people reading this are nodding or smiling in agreement. Many of us have experienced that magical email telling us to log into a system to update our banking details urgently, failing which we would miss payroll. Now think to yourself, what tangible value do I get in learning a process that I will probably use once in my career at this company? I understand the intrinsic value (getting paid).

Now imagine if Amazon expected you to learn how to get to the checkout each time things changed. Oh wait, they don't. They created the 1-Click checkout.

Let's overlay this in a world with a mix of users of varying digital IQs, where users rightfully expect digital experiences that blend with their own digital realities. Yet despite this, many organizations continue to provide homogeneous learning experiences, mostly because it's cheaper and easier. Never mind if it doesn't actually solve the problems it's designed to address, namely getting users to use the software.

Earlier I talked about needing to evolve to a 21st century mindset. Now imagine if organizations used the same insights and tech muscle on their overwhelmed employees. The challenge starts with a serious conflict of outcomes where the theory of the transformation trumps the impact of its reality.

Remember, the shift to cloud computing and agile software development has meant a flood of new programs and tasks for users to learn. What's more, they have less time between updates and new releases to learn and become proficient with their new skills. In essence, this means they are drowning in waves of launch, train, forget, update, train, forget, and so on in an endless cycle of learning and forgetting.

When you put all those layers on the user, then blend them with the forgetting curve and the learning curve, it's easy to see how it creates a sense of being overwhelmed.

"But wait," as the man says, "there's more!"

Thanks to a global pandemic, we're all working from home (in some form or another). Some of us will continue to do so long after the pandemic has subsided.

Working from home presents a different set of challenges. It used to be you would go to your day job. You would have your morning commute where you might be surfing the web or chatting with someone. You get to the office, put away your things. You would log onto your company's network. Maybe you would have a conversation with a nearby coworker.

Maybe get up from your desk and walk down the hall to get a cup of coffee. Chit chat with someone about their weekend. Soon, you would have your first meeting of the day. After that, take a break. Go to another meeting. Then probably have another coffee break. Then another meeting before doing a bit of work.

Go to lunch, come back. Maybe finish off a PowerPoint. Have another break. Have another meeting. By the end of the day, you've probably done four hours of proper work. And even then, in those pre-COVID-19 days, you felt overwhelmed by incoming information and new things to learn.

Now, fast forward to this new way of working where you don't have the commute. You're likely in front of your desk by eight o'clock. You jump right into your work. No stroll to get coffee or morning chitchat with a coworker. Maybe you have a 20-minute lunch break (okay, maybe 10-minute) before your afternoon gets stacked up again with work and video conference calls.

If you keep doing that, you're going to hit a wall. You won't be as productive. You're going to struggle.

What's more, that sense of being overwhelmed is just going to stack up as you go through each day. Not surprisingly, it's going to manifest itself in the way workers talk about their jobs and how they talk about each other. And make no mistake, there's what people say...and there's what they mean.

They say: "I don't have enough time in the day."

They mean: "I'm consumed by email."

They say: "I can't find the application."

They mean: "I'm flooded with new digital processes I have to learn."

They say: "I'm in—now what do I do?"

They mean: "I forgot what to do already. Don't judge me!"

They say: "I can't find what you need me to do!"

They mean: "The software implementation was not elegant."

If you're anything like me, the negative effects of being overwhelmed can go far beyond productivity. Over time, these forces can erode your confidence in your abilities to keep up and, thus, to do your job.

In my experience that can lead to insecurity and anxiety around your position and your ability to provide for yourself and those you support. That hardly adds up to an ideal and productive employee.

This is why companies have a vested interest in devising strategies that reduce their employees' feeling of being overwhelmed. And quickly. They need strategies and tools that help people be the most productive version of themselves and adapt to whatever comes along in this ever-changing environment. That's where a DAP comes in.

A DAP provides users relief from this sense of being overwhelmed by serving almost like a concierge service helping users with the corporate process throughout their workday. It is the release valve on the pressure cooker.

And, because of all the varying digital IQs, one of the keys to a DAP's success is its ability to be there when and where a workforce with varying digital IQs needs help.

While I said earlier it's naive to assume older users have a lower digital IQ than younger users, there are differences between the two types of users.

For instance, anecdotal data gleaned from customer interactions suggest that older users generally log onto systems earlier in the morning than their younger coworkers. This stems in part from a generational belief that the so-called "productive hours" of the day are meant to be interacting with human beings rather than technology.

But if older workers are going to dive in between 6:30 a.m. and 8:00 a.m., that means they're going to need digital help before help desk support is actually available during business hours.

My experience tells me that millennials—typically night owls who are most productive at night—aren't going to be up at 7:00 a.m. Heck, he or she probably didn't even get to bed until the early morning. Instead, our millennial user is going to be working at 10:00 p.m. and needs frictionless technical support at that time.

And what about those rapid, unceasing stomach-churning waves of changes brought about by cloud-based computing and Agile development? A DAP can relieve the relentless pounding on users' anxiety.

Rather than launch, train, forget, update, train, forget, etc., where companies essentially keep moving peoples' cheese, a DAP helps normalize the amplitudes and frequency of these waves in a way that is truly life-changing in the corporate world. No longer are updates a cause for anxiety. People aren't asked to learn and retain new functions in some learning center, only to be released back to their workspace and expect to remember it all.

Instead, a DAP helps users execute and learn in real-time as they are working. In this way, a DAP distills all the noise and rockiness because ultimately when you need to do something and do it right, it literally says to the user, "Here you go, this is what you need to do, and here's how you need to do it."

It calms the waves of change, so to speak. And that sense of calm brings reassurance and confidence, both of which dial back that sense of being overwhelmed just a little bit. If a company does that every day, a little bit, then it has a positive impact on what its workforce is doing.

Therein lies the simple promise of a DAP: To make things better for technology users so they can help the company achieve better business outcomes. But like good parents, we should take a good look at what a DAP really is before we put our user babies in the care of one.

DAP Dos

Where do you stand in the debate of the overwhelmed employee? Before you answer the question, think about some of the points raised in this chapter:

- Do you feel compelled to stack your day with meetings?
- Do you struggle with Zoom fatigue?
- Have you baked multiple time-out sessions in your day to pause, breathe, and reflect?
- Are you constantly checking your cell phone for a new work email or text?
- Are you looking at email over the weekend or at 8:00 p.m. at night?

Now, take a moment to speak with your staff. Chances are many of them are in this bucket. If they are, it may be time to think about some intervention events where a DAP can help. Like the old British Telecom (BT) commercial put it, "It's good to talk."

CHAPTER 6

WHAT IS A DAP, ANYWAY?

A s we walked away from the schoolyard, both my wife Sarina and I were beginning to feel a quiet calm that we had done the right thing. Ari had now completed his third year of preschool and it was clear he was no longer crawling; in most areas he was walking if not running, figuratively speaking.

Ari was two years old and we had decided to immerse him in Mandarin by putting him in a Chinese-speaking preschool. I remember his first few months vividly. Each day, he sprinted to his mum or me holding on for dear life as if we had left him to fend for himself in a den of lions. He was petrified of his surroundings, probably wondering what he did to deserve this fate.

Fast-forward to 2021 and here is a kid, now six years old, and who has no Mandarin support at home, yet is so fluent that he is the chief speaker when we dine out at Chinese restaurants. He orders everything down to the small details of a small spoon and fork to accommodate his tiny hands, a small glass of warm water, not forgetting a large dish of soy sauce, which is still the standard accessory with his bowl of rice.

To this day, his mother and I sit in amazement at how this child has managed (and continues) to navigate through this complex language. When we break it down, he has had a personal concierge with him every step of the way. But more of that later.

As I discussed in Chapter 5, we don't start out our digital lives as overwhelmed users. Our environment shapes us to be that way.

Even earlier in this book, I suggested that any organization wishing to give its employees technology to use to drive the business forward would do well to think of those people as baby users. And I made the case that DAPs help baby users become more independent users.

There are distinct parallels here, so indulge me in the baby user metaphor for a moment. We actually start our digital lives much as we do our real lives: As babies with a great amount of potential, but zero mastery.

Just as you can't hand a baby a manual and say, "Good luck!" you can't turn loose baby users either. You have to teach them to crawl, to walk, and then run on their own if you ever want them to be productive. You have to teach them to navigate their world before he or she can become independent.

For instance, say you want a baby to cross a room. First, you have to teach him or her to crawl. Then you introduce the notion of standing. Each of us parents can remember the comedic scene of our baby propping him or herself up before shaky legs give way beneath them. In the beginning, he or she is unsteady and needs assistance. Eventually, they learn to stand on their own and take their initial wobbly steps. They fall.

They get back up.

They try again, this time grasping for something to hold onto. Eventually, they progress to walking on their own. From there, the pace picks up as walking transforms into running.

Let's say, if left to learn on his or her own, it takes a baby six and a half minutes to crawl across a room. What if you could move that baby from crawling directly to sprinting? What if you could reduce the time it takes to cross the room to a mere 70 seconds?

That's what a DAP does for our baby users. It takes them from a crawling use of technology to a sprinting one in a remarkably short period of time. They learn quickly by doing. And they learn so much faster and over so many different obstacle courses (platforms and applications) that I maintain that using a DAP isn't a new way of training; it's a new way of working.

A DAP helps our baby user become more independent and successful, more resilient. It makes them feel smarter, more confident. And it does this much faster than traditional (training) methods, according to what we've learned from using DAPs. And when I say fast, I mean blazingly fast. Usain Bolt fast.

Let's say the six and a half minutes it takes a real baby to crawl across a room is also how long it takes a baby user on average to complete a web form on a page. First of all, let me point out that before DAPs and the usage information they provide, we didn't even know that.

Now let's say the baby user has to complete three forms. That's 20 minutes of the baby user's life.

On top of that, let's assume the baby will struggle with inputting data on the form. Picture the scene where the baby user tries once and gets an error message. He tries again and again before doing what all kids do—fudge the answer so they can move on to the next part of the puzzle.

That's what the baby user does too. He leaves the form or enters bad information just to get through the form. This is where one of the pillars of digital transformations fails.

You see, most programs are sold on the realization of a combination of five business objectives: driving self-service, improving data quality, reducing support costs, ensuring better compliance, and leveraging insights for continuous process improvement. And here at the start of the journey, already we are confronted with the baby trying to circumnavigate one of the outcomes we laid out in the original business case.

Also, let's say it takes our baby users 10 steps to complete all these forms. If for some reason the baby user has to take more than 10 steps, every additional step brings the baby user that much closer to saying, "That's it. I've done enough" and stopping. In fact, the data tells us abandonment rates go up as high as 50 percent when the process takes 10 steps or more.[80]

When we use a DAP to guide the baby user through the forms, we find that the ideal time spent completing a process is a mere *70 seconds*.[81]

What's more, error rates decline to almost zero. This means the data gathered is accurate, thus reducing the time someone else has to spend fixing the errors. Additionally, abandonment rates fall considerably.

Think of it: Baby users learning to use their tools faster and more accurately. All because a DAP is there helping the baby user through the process.

A Digital Adoption Platform

It's important to understand that a digital adoption platform is, in fact, a platform. It is not a set of help bubbles that pops up on the screen. It's not a question mark you click on to get more information. In short, it is not Clippy (the discontinued Microsoft Office assistant in the form of a paperclip). Essentially, a DAP merges an array of functionality to take away the friction from how a baby user engages with technology to get the outcome they desire.

It does this by combining data about user actions and engagement elements with onscreen guidance capabilities that can be updated based on user behavior analytics. That is, it helps you see what users are struggling with and gives you the tools to smooth out the bumps in the road where baby users are having trouble.

And because it needs to work wherever a baby user needs to work, a DAP is there to act as a concierge of sorts for the baby user as they try to navigate everything from external websites, internal corporate applications, native mobile applications; even from the desktop of the baby user. In short, it shouldn't judge what playground the baby user finds himself in. It should just work.

---

80 "WalkMe Unveils Unprecedented Data Highlighting Where Employees Struggle in Business Processes," Cision, April 10, 2019, https://www.prnewswire.com/news-releases/walkme-unveils-unprecedented-data-highlighting-where-employees-struggle-in-business-processes-300829801.html.

81 Ibid.

How a DAP Works

First and foremost, a DAP is a technology-agnostic layer that sits on top of any digital asset. Think of it as the plastic screen protector we use on our mobile phones. In the most technical sense, a DAP can be deployed through a browser extension or embedded into applications similar to how Google analytics is installed. In this way it's like that screen protector, meaning you can overlay the benefits of a DAP rather than having to try to integrate it deep within an organization's existing enterprise software. A DAP integration is, relatively speaking, unobtrusive, quick, and clean.

Once put into place, the DAP comes alive. As soon as the technology is deployed, the DAP begins to aggregate and arrange data points into meaningful insights. Dashboards form, allowing departments to understand what applications are being used, how often they are being used, and for how long. The traditional needle in the haystack suddenly becomes a simpler proposition because we can now decide which haystack we want to tackle first.

With time (and I mean each minute, hour, and day), these data points grow. These data points serve as minute journey points. And as the DAP pieces each of these together, patterns form. Some patterns are remarkably consistent between users, but other more complex patterns begin to emerge shining the light on how different users, without any supervision, may meander through systems often not reaching the desired destination.

The easiest way to think of a DAP is to imagine the humble GPS. Whether you use Garmin, Google Maps, or Waze, I think we have all benefited from the smarts and simplicity these devices and applications have afforded us. They have become such a core part of our lives that outside of hitting the ignition button in our car dashboards and plugging in the seatbelt, punching in our destination is probably one of the next three things we tend to do when we get into our cars or as we come off the subway.

The question is why? Probably because we have experienced the value of the science of the technology. Remember the time you needed to get to that meeting across town and you knew you didn't have any margin for error in terms of travel time. You knew the quickest way there was via the freeway but you simply didn't know how to get to the entrance.

And when you did, remember the sigh of relief when Hilda (everyone names their GPS don't they?) preempts you to stick to the left lane because there is an accident on the right lane, and imagine your bemusement when Hilda prompts you to take the next exit because you missed your turn. Now as you take the exit Hilda begins to rethink your journey, understanding where you are and adjusting to automating different routes each with an understanding of how long it will take you to get there.

In the old days, our options would have been limited to maybe jumping into a cab and getting stuck in traffic, or perhaps we would have been limited to the traditional map. When I was studying in England, this used to be called the A-Z street atlas. During my time in grad school in Melbourne, the Melway was the guide. The challenge with the old paper-based maps was that you had to keep buying new versions as a city's urban landscape changed. They didn't work cross-state. The beauty of a DAP is that like our digital GPS, it works for drivers across state lines, a DAP accompanies and guides baby users across sites and applications both internal and external.

Functionally speaking, there are three layers to the ways a DAP helps users: smart guidance, proactive engagement, and process automation.

Now that sounds like a lot of jargon, but when you put yourself in the baby user's shoes, it makes common sense.

Smart Guidance

This is very much like using a GPS. You simply punch in where you want to go, and the DAP begins to calibrate and then gives you directions. A GPS tells you things like, turn left here, turn right there. It also works when you cross state lines, it tells you when you've made a wrong turn and how to correct your course.

That's part of what a DAP does. The user literally opens up the DAP and instead of typing in where they want to go, users type in what they want to do (e.g., fill out an order form, complete an HR task, pay an invoice, etc.)

The DAP calibrates, then guides the user to the application they need to complete the task. And like the GPS working across state lines, a DAP can work on internal sites and applications as well as external platforms the user needs to use.

Now the smart part is where the elements of the journey become complex like trying to complete a process that requires multiple forms or using multiple applications. Imagine you are trying to buy some travel insurance. The first couple of steps are straightforward; name, address, age, gender, etc. Then the first BIG question: Do you have any preexisting health conditions?

If the answer is no, then it is simple. If the answer is yes, then here is where the complexity arises: Is it life-threatening?

If no, great. If yes, when was the last episode? Were you hospitalized? For how long? Did you need specialist care? Do you have your doctor's notes? Can you upload them?

Each of these branches presents a different level of complexity often leading the user to quit the process because of the sense of being overwhelmed.

Proactive Engagement

Don't put off to tomorrow what you can do today. Ever been told this? As people, we typically put off things that we deem as unimportant or challenging. Think about the annual performance review or goal-setting process. Both have strategic importance to a company, but if we measured the effort organizations put into the completion of these two simple processes, I think we would be amazed.

The assessment period is typically open for a month where an email is sent out to all employees by someone important in the organization. But given we're all overwhelmed by all the amount of email we get, we typically ignore this first call to action. Fast forward three weeks and management get a report highlighting that only 37 percent of employees have completed their annual reviews.

The immediate reaction is to send out another email. Okay, we got a 5 percent bump. Time to rethink the approach. Each delinquent employee now gets a call from his or her line manager.

Okay, now we are up to 50 percent. What else can we do?

When in doubt, bring in the big guns and get a senior leader to send a voice note either on the corporate intranet page, or have all the executives' personal assistants call each individual.

At the end of the process, many times, the end goal hasn't been achieved in that having all employees complete their appraisals. If we do get there, the actual content may be subpar because users have done it begrudgingly and if the system experience isn't simple, this tends to exacerbate the quality of the input.

Now imagine a world where no emails are sent. No calls. No video messages. No hysteria. The DAP world is simple. Because of the analytics, we now know where users spend their time so we can send a pop up on that specific screen saying, "Hey, it's that time of year again, we need you to complete your annual appraisals in order for us to get your bonus payments right. Please click here."

We know some will click on the button while others will ignore it, but this time you know who hasn't completed the process and so you send the same message. Now with 24 hours to go, instead of the dramatic calls, etc., this time that targeted message pops up on that person's screen...but this time it freezes the screen, forcing the user to do what is expected of them. Only this time the smart guidance reduces the pain where the digital assistant or DAP guides the user with the elegance of a professional ballerina. This reality exists.

Process Automation

Almost every company I work with has some form of Robotics Process Automation program either in flight or pending. The thing with RPA is that it was designed for a robot to launch and execute basic, repetitive tasks typically on a large scale.

In a DAP world, process automation takes a different form given that the journey may require human interventions mid-flow. The DAP helps with process automation by actually having the ability to take over parts of

WHAT IS A DAP, ANYWAY?

a process that the organization recognizes can be automated.

Here is a very real example: One of the key reasons companies decide to undergo digital transformations is to improve the quality of data in their systems for better decision-making or compliance reasons. One morning I received a phone call from one of my prospects. She was flustered and emotional. You see, they had just lost an employee. He lost his life on the job, and they had no way of getting in contact with his wife, emergency contact, and next of kin because the new HR system they spent millions of dollars implementing didn't have the information. Only weeks before, each employee had been asked to update their information, but many didn't because they simply didn't know how.

With a DAP, all the user had to do would be to click on a link and the automation would kick in, transporting the user to the exact page where the details were needed. In basic baby user language, the DAP would screen-skip through the irrelevant pages landing the baby user at the right end-point *and* validating that the information that was updated was accurate.

Putting It All Together

For a DAP to add real value, it needs to be able to blend these three functional layers, applying them on demand when the user needs a specific type of assistance.

For instance, let's say there's a lengthy form a person has to use every time they want to work with a new vendor. First, they have to get the vendor on the approved vendor list. This may be a four-form, 100-step process requiring 125 data points.

Once that's done, they then have to complete another process to open a purchase order for the work the vendor is providing to the company. This may entail several other forms and inputs taking several hours to prepare and several people to approve. And remember, that's just one job with one vendor.

Rather than having to complete this process for every new vendor and the purchase order for every job a vendor does, a DAP could streamline this process. The baby user types what they want to do (e.g., add the vendor to the approved vendor list). The DAP could start an online chat with the baby user, asking questions to get the required information, in essence breaking down the tedious nature of filling out forms into a simple conversation.

The DAP could then take the baby user's conversation and automatically place it into the required fields of the forms. Once done, the DAP would then proactively reach out to the baby user asking the baby user if they needed to open a purchase order.

If so, the DAP could re-use the information the baby users already provided about the vendor to complete the purchase order and speed up the process. A DAP would also identify where new or different information was required and prompt the baby user to provide it rather than submit an incomplete request. The DAP would also validate the information as it's being given.

A DAP can also act as a sort of concierge, reminding the user of tasks they need to complete. A good example of this might be onboarding a new employee.

Imagine it is my first day at work. A new challenge, a new opportunity, a new platform for me to really strut my stuff. I sit down at my desk (most likely in my home office), switch on my laptop, and my first digital experience is a welcome email, thanking me for my decision to invest my time with the company. It also provides a collection of links to applications that I may need in the distant future.

I am asked to complete some logistical tasks namely updating my banking information before the last day of the month so I can get paid, updating my zip code so my payroll tax calculation will be accurate, making sure my emergency contact information is up to date before making a requisition for a company mobile phone.

Seems simple enough right? But for a baby user, new to the organization, this can be daunting. Where are these applications? How do I find the username and password? Okay, now that I am in, what do I do? Where do I click? Is there a guide I need to read? Maybe there is a link in that original email? Okay, got the guide, why does the guide look so different from the application? It was published in August 2018, that's why.

An hour in and I am no further along. The enthusiasm of my first day and the week has waned.

For many executives, they will never go through this journey because they have the luxury of a personal assistant who is either an expert user or plugged into a network of expert users. So why can't we all have a personal assistant?

With a DAP, everyone gets a digital assistant who initiates the process, then guides the baby user through the process. It takes them to the first form to be completed—all the while checking the user enters the correct information, then skips screens (code for automation) and takes the user to the next application or form that needs to be completed.

All in all, helping the user execute on the process tasks in significantly less time than it would take them stumbling around on their own and with no errors because the DAP has been validating data and data formats along the way.

Through a combination of guidance, engagement, and automation, the DAP makes the process less tedious and much faster than the typical process where the user completes the forms question-by-question, if they complete it at all.

Why a DAP Works

Like so many tools and platforms, a DAP works not merely because of the bits and bytes but because of the context in which all the elements are applied. We shared some basic examples above, but I wanted to dive a little deeper.

Whilst a DAP comprises a GPS-like functional layer blended with process automation capabilities sitting on top of a rich insights engine that can aggregate usage from an element level to an end-to-end process to an application stack, what sets it apart are four additional complementary elements.

1. A content curation tool that has been designed for a functional (not technical) user allowing the curator to design, deploy, and augment the user journey. Meaning it needs to be easy to use and if you need help it has its own in-built DAP.

2. An extension platform that compliments the content curation tool with templates, best practices, and innovations that accelerate value realization for customers. If a process like applying for time off is the same system-wide then why can't we leverage templated content?

3. A machine learning algorithm that learns with each use. If you think about it, what we are trying to do is to get this GPS-like experience to work on different machines configured in different ways, operating on different operating systems, and being accessed on different browsers. The permutations are huge, so much so that the DAP must be a learning platform so that it learns from its mistakes (when content breaks).

4. Content curators who appreciate that they need to think about different types of users when they build content. The reactive user may well need to be cajoled, guided to complete a process. The proactive user may simply want a conversation experience. Each of these user types may well need the same content to help them but presented in a different way. A way that makes it a little more human.

A DAP works so well because it's actively engaging with the user. In some ways, it takes the core of a GPS and brings it into the baby user's everyday work life.

Much like a GPS doesn't just give you direction but also warns of things like stalled traffic ahead, construction, etc., and then reroutes you, a DAP isn't waiting for questions from the baby user. Instead, it's guiding them through the process, reminding them of tasks they need to complete while simplifying the tedious parts of the processes with automation.

In the same way that a GPS doesn't drive the car for you, a DAP isn't doing the work for your baby users. Instead, it's giving them the ability to navigate the digital tasks and processes, so they complete their work more quickly, more accurately, and more efficiently.

I would go so far as to suggest a definition of digital adoption to be: "The technology's ability to proactively engage a user at the time of need and to help him execute the digital processes accurately without additional assistance in a timely manner."

Again, employing a DAP in your organization means more than a new way of learning. It's a revolution. It's part of the transformation. The paradigm is no longer learning the flow of work but successfully executing the flow of work. This is the revolution in how learning and working are done within your organization.

This is because a DAP goes beyond helping baby users. It also helps your organization identify the parts of your digital processes giving your baby users the most trouble. Maybe a section takes too long to complete. Or perhaps a significant number of users drop off at a particular field in the process.

Now, we've all seen the stats that say how often our users fail. But the stats don't say specifically where they've failed. It's easy to say we failed because of the user or we failed because of the technology.

With a DAP you can be more precise about where processes are failing. It can tell you that, say, 63 percent of your baby users are falling off in step five of a 14-step process. Now we can visually see a representation of how and why 30 or 40 percent of different people in a particular step fall off just because a button is in the wrong (new) place.

From an analytics perspective, a DAP can help you reconstruct and correct the parts of your technology process that are causing friction for your baby users. By identifying these friction points, a DAP allows the company to quickly create DAP content that smooths over these friction points for the baby users.

This content is created through a content curation tool built into the DAP. It allows the company to quickly create digital conversations, instructions, and other helpful content to ease the baby user through the spots that are giving them trouble. This reduces user frustration and makes more efficient use of their time.

The organization can see where their process challenges are because they have all their technology usage on one dashboard. They can see how many users are using all their different technology and how often. As well as helping the company identify and remove obstacles, it can inform future technology buying needs.

Five General Use Cases

When you think about digital transformation journeys, there are generally five common pit stops you should consider along the way to reaching a true digital transformation:

1. Insights first
2. System onboarding
3. Just-in-time help
4. New software releases and functional updates
5. Support tickets

Fail to succeed at any one of these pit stops in your journey and you are practically guaranteed to fail. But hit them all and you'll realize the promised value that convinced senior stakeholders to invest millions of dollars in the program in the first place. A bit like the learning-forgetting curve discussion we had earlier, it has become evident that a gap exists between the value realization promise and the reality. If we took the time to rethink the following pit stops with the use of a DAP, companies are likely to give themselves a better chance of success.

Insights First

If your baby users are already engaging with the software, would it be smart to peel back the layers to see where they are falling down, giving up, or simply stuck. Remember that the moment you deploy the DAP you have the ability to begin to uncover the mess made by the babies and then figuring out which mess would add the most value. If you know that putting a piece of candy next to a particular field would get you 30 percent more babies into that happy place, then you have a BIG solution. And fewer crying babies.

System Onboarding

This is about how you introduce your new technology to your baby users. The old method was some version of hauling people into a classroom or onto a web-based training session, walking them through the applications, then sending them back to forget most of it what you showed them within the first 24 hours.

With a DAP, as we've shown, the learning takes place while doing in the application. When your baby user makes a mistake, the DAP is there to correct it. When the baby user doesn't know where to go next, the DAP points them in the right direction. It speeds up the learning process, the executing process, blurring the lines between training and working.

Add to this the fact that we are reducing the burden of having multiple trainers, set training times, and not knowing which babies have truly understood, we have kind of rethought the whole idea of preschool to home-school with the added benefit of smiling happy little people.

Just-in-Time Help

This is perhaps the biggest advantage of using DAP to make your digital transformation. The old way, as we discussed with my missing or moved button, was for a stuck user to ask someone for help. Could be the person next to them, could be a specialist staffing a help desk. Now the friction point is taking up the time of at least two employees for a single problem.

The user might decide to self-serve their issue, spending (wasting?) time searching through an online knowledge base. Assuming they can come up with the correct wording and the information is, in fact, in the knowledge base, the user might have their solution within...um...several minutes? That is, if the user doesn't simply give up after a couple of fruitless attempts.

But baby users working within a DAP find comfort and confidence knowing that help is always there on screen at the exact moment when the individual user needs it. The DAP is always present in the background, waiting to be summoned by the baby user. Or, if a lengthy amount of time passes between on-screen activity, the DAP can step in to ask the baby user if they need help with the task at hand.

Because the company has analyzed the baby usage data from their DAP, they can easily identify where users are having trouble and create onscreen instructions to address them as they happen.

Again, this just-in-time help is there no matter when or where baby users—all of differing digital IQs, remember—need assistance. This holds true whether it's late at night when the help desk is unattended, or the wee hours of the morning as one generation wakes and rises, passing in the hallway a younger generation only now wandering off to sleep.

New Software Releases and Functional Updates

Much like death and taxes in the physical world, in the software world the only thing certain is change. Most cloud applications have between two to four major functional releases each year. No matter how they are dressed up, these are changes that will impact the user.

Let's assume for a moment that each application includes innovations or user experience updates which may result in a user needing to learn how the application has changed in 10 ways.

Now let's assume we have four applications. That makes 40 new things to learn or remember.

Now let's multiply that by four times a year because these are quarterly in nature. Now we are at 160 changes a year and counting. My button merely shifted from the bottom right to the top left and just that one little thing caused a bunch of drama. Imagine the dramas that will stir when the baby user can't find the rattle, ball, or teddy bear.

Support Tickets

The quickest way to impact the P&L of an organization is to figure out how to reduce the cost to serve its customer. No matter how well you teach people or how often you train and retrain them, people forget. That means all this digital innovation and speed is causing speed bumps for the people making the journey on your digital transformation.

And not just for the baby users. It's draining your support staff resources and driving up support costs.

Let's revisit my missing or moved button example with some round numbers to show the effects on the P&L sheet. Say the help desk takes 1,000 calls a month. That's 12,000 a year.

Now let's say a third of those calls are from people like me who want to know why the button is missing when in fact it's only just moved to a different part of the screen. That's 4,000 calls a year on this one issue.

Now let's assume each of those calls cost $25 to handle. That's $75,000 a year to handle a change that a DAP can easily fix by simply pointing the baby users to the button's new screen location at the different yet exact moments all your different baby users need to click the button they can't find. That's one expensive button.

It's in these areas that a DAP allows you to rethink how your baby users are learning and working. But it does something even more impressive than that: A DAP helps you rethink *who* is doing the learning and working.

Three years on, we sit as proud parents as our son, Ari, continues to amaze us with his mastery of the Chinese language. While he is not yet a black belt in the language, his confidence, vocabulary, and ability to converse in coherent sentences are the result of having a personal concierge (a teacher) with props (guidance and engagement) to smooth out his journey to date. For a five-year-old, he is sprinting.

As the new school year begins it will be interesting to see if he stumbles through the potholes, whether he slows down to a walk or if the new character sets force him back to a crawl. What is clear is that having his personal concierge provides him with confidence, trust, guile, and drive.

DAP Dos

These questions might be worth discussing at your next team meeting:

- Is your organization trying to impact your operational goals by positively improving how well your employees are doing with the five use cases laid out above?

- Are you able to measure the impact each is having on the productivity of your employees?

- Is the impact (or lack thereof) being translated to cashable benefits?

- Have you thought about the impact of the five pit stops could have on your cross-department processes?

CHAPTER 7

HERO WANTED

Joe Atkinson, chief digital officer at PwC and one of the sharpest thinkers in the digital world, once asked this biting question during a WalkMe webinar: "Would we blame the customer for the lack of performance the same way we do our employees?"[82]

I think that if we are honest, many organizations view the employee experience as the last customer of the organization. This mindset has resulted in a spaghetti-like mess often resulting in lower-than-expected performance. Our retort is to blame the employee for not leveraging the tools that we have provided him.

Now imagine if we produced a product for a customer and it didn't sell. We would have postmortem, look for root cause analysis and, in some cases, this catastrophe could be career limiting. As leaders, if we want digital transformations to stick, we need to be obsessed with creating world-class experiences for our employees, not just our paying customers.

If we treated them like our most important customers, we would lower the risk of failure. We would raise the likelihood that employees would embrace the new digital changes, because the experience value of making work better, lives easier, exceeding expectations, will drive the change.

---

82   Amir Farhi and Joe Atkinson, "Turning Crisis into Opportunity: Giving Employees the Digital Experience They Deserve," WalkMe/PwC, accessed May 14, 2021, https://www.walkme.com/webinars/remote-employee-pwc/.

Knowing that you have a chance of winning will keep the employee on the same court as opposed to taking his game to a shadow arena simply because it is easier.

More critically, this need is growing on a daily basis. Like the annual danger of accumulating water pressure pressing on China's Three Gorges Dam, waves of digital change put exponential pressure on organizations and their employees. Today, we have already passed that point where organizations that don't address the need for this paradigm shift will fall further behind. We need to act fast, and we need a bunch of superheroes.

In comic books, superheroes always turn up to save the day. But to save the day, they need relevant superpowers. Some measurements are more obvious than others. Stopping a speeding train heading for a cliff? Pretty clear-cut.

Yet there is no point in having super speed when what is required is super precision. In short, can our superhero exceed expectations or her objectives? If she can do so and consistently, then the title hero and the expectation of saving the day are apt.

As I've laid out, a DAP teaches baby users to crawl, walk, and run quickly in terms of using their digital tools. But what if I told you the potential is even greater? What if these baby users, with the assistance of a DAP, can grow into superheroes?

In truth, a DAP holds the potential to empower people, organizations, and their leadership to go from merely crawling to launching themselves into the air like superheroes (metaphorically speaking, of course), accelerating the new way of working that you intended in the first place when you embarked on your digital transformation journey.

No matter what industry you're in, getting your baby users to perform like superheroes with the right tools should be your priority. It's an overarching factor with competitive ramifications for businesses across all industries.

According to a survey of 500 CIOs conducted by Constellation Research, digital transformation topped all other priorities (77.3 percent), including cybersecurity, among IT professionals as they headed into 2021.[83] According to Dion Hinchcliffe, vice president and principal analyst at Constellation, "the data shows that CIOs will be seeking dramatic improvements from their IT investments."[84]

Hinchcliffe goes on to point out that employee mental health is a key concern. Workers becoming more remote, more siloed, more disconnected from the organization, frustrated by technical challenges of current infrastructure, and potentially overwhelmed by new processes—all these obstacles are in play because of the "new normal" brought on by the pandemic. It has placed a huge spotlight on the remote worker, as opposed to initial tech strategies that didn't think about the remote worker as the core persona of the digital transformation.

As we've seen, the prospects of a successful digital transformation without a DAP are quite dismal. But does the needle truly shift with a DAP in place? I'm happy to say Forrester Research conducted an in-depth exercise across four distinctly different organizations (Red Hat, Inc., CHRISTUS Health, Modernizing Medicine, and Engie) with some illuminating results.

These four organizations reported several key benefits including a reduction in training time (60 percent), savings in IT help desk tickets (50 percent), and savings in software licensing fees (20 percent).[85]

Diving deeper when putting the lens on customer-facing services, the findings included a 35 percent increase in customer retention, upsell growth from existing customers of 10 percent, and savings in customer support costs by as much as 50 percent. Tobias Washington, head of talent technologies at CHRISTUS Health which was part of the research, estimated an 80–90 percent cost savings on training after implementing a DAP.[86]

The in-depth analysis published in an October 2020 report confirmed

83   WalkMe, "Digital Transformation Is the Number One Budget Priority for Fortune 500 CIOs in 2021," Cision, December 1, 2020, https://www.prnewswire.com/il/news-releases/digital-transformation-is-the-number-one-budget-priority-for-fortune-500-cios-in-2021-301182396.html.

84   Dion Hinchcliffe, WalkMe, "CIO Perspective" YouTube video.

85   WalkMe, "Forrester Analysis Found a Three-Year 368% ROI with WalkMe," accessed May 14, 2021, https://www.walkme.com/pages/forrester-tei-study/?t=19&eco=TEI&camp=TEI&abt1=7014G000001GN5J.

86   WalkMe, "How to Win Digital Transformation in the Post-COVID Era: TEI Confirms 368% ROI over 3 Years with Digital Adoption," Cision, November 10, 2020, https://www.prnewswire.com/il/news-releases/how-to-win-digital-transformation-in-the-post-covid-era-tei-confirms-368-roi-over-3-years-with-digital-adoption-301169706.html.

a 368 percent ROI in a payback period of less than three months with a present value of benefits exceeding $20 million over three years.[87]

In short, a DAP not only worked across a range of operational levers but had an impact quickly. That $20 million was spread across reduced costs in customer support and software licensing along with increased revenue from shorter sales cycles as well as increases in user retention, upselling, application usage, and process efficiency.

In other words, a DAP not only helps you transform digitally, but in doing so it positively affects the economics of your organization. Remember the caterpillar metamorphosing into the flighty butterfly?

Of course, not all DAPs are created equal, and results will vary from DAP solution to DAP solution. Nor are all organizations the same. What is apparent, though, is that implementing a DAP is key to successfully transforming your baby users into digital superheroes to achieve your organization's goals.

As with comic books, if we're trying to get a baby user to be a superhero, we first need to understand what superpower they need. Having a measurable destination is key if you're going to have any legitimate hopes of ever getting there.

For instance, do we know what the baby user's baseline is? How does a shift in that baseline affect the organization's profit and loss? Who will it impact? And perhaps most importantly, *what is the impact of* not *fixating on the baby user's baseline?*

Before we can get baby users to take off into the sky in terms of their proficiency and effectiveness with the digital tools that they need for their jobs, we need to understand what would constitute success for them. Is it about completing the process successfully? Is it about completing the process in a shorter time or perhaps completing the process consistently over a period of time? Or all of the above.

To be truly successful companies need to shift from training people to be "better, faster" to instead identifying and measuring how they can impact business and financial metrics. If you're setting out on your transfor-

87   WalkMe, "Forrester Analysis."

mation journey, it's incredibly important to think about your destination and what "good" looks like before you start. The question you need to be fixated on is: *Where do you want to end up?*

Value Frameworks

First and foremost, it's important to be clear on the outcomes you are trying to achieve. For instance, if you are a retailer, be clear about the metrics you are trying to hit. Also consider the implications to traditional store expectations.

Or if you are a bank, perhaps rethinking traditional brick-and-mortar processes and trying digital self-service processes allows you by default to rethink the staff mix in a retail branch. This might allow a bank to move to a smaller space or do away with branches altogether while improving its balance sheet.

For Z Energy, a fuel company in New Zealand, rethinking the driver experience when filling up a tank of petrol was an important innovation step during their COVID-19 experience. They recreated a customer journey that leveraged contactless payments using your license plate as you pulled into the gas station. It was so seamless that any driver of any generation found the process as simple as driving in, letting a camera identify your vehicle, pumping, and leaving.[88]

But each of these transformations above needs some guide rails to ensure value is realized. Introducing the value framework.

Your value framework will keep you honest and, if leveraged correctly, will determine if you're getting the value you set out to attain from your transformation program. Value frameworks are designed to connect business objectives with key performance indicators. Success should impact operational goals. There are many value frameworks out there, which is why it's important to know yours at the beginning of your transformation. In simple terms, you should always be looking for simple value statement, for example:

---

88 Pablo Plaza, "Z Energy Introduces NZ-first Pay by Number Plate Option," PetrolPlaza, December 4, 2020, https://www.petrolplaza.com/news/26132.

"I want to reduce support tickets from our Top 10 issues by 20 percent by the end of the year."

or

"I want to increase paid conversions from 10 percent to 30 percent by Q3 this year."

By understanding where you are, where you want to get to, and by when, you can begin to build out intervention events that focus your organization on how best to get to the goal.

For example, if you're a telecommunications provider, your transformation may be to improve to your net promoter score. How do you reduce the friction to your services for customers?

Or maybe it's how do you transform into a consumer player rather than just the provider of a pipeline?

Or if you were just a run-of-the-mill organization, it might be, how do you become more efficient and more effective?

Just as there are many frameworks out there, there are a number of things to measure. Many of them are the "better, faster" metrics tied to what we traditionally think of as business goals (profit, loss, growth, etc.). Others are tied less directly to "better, faster" metrics but it's nearly impossible to experience any sort of sustained better, faster results without them.

Take, for instance, setting a baseline for measuring employee engagement or health. This is about trying to measure their happiness. This is hardly a traditional business metric, but don't think it isn't top of mind for most of the technology leaders as some of the world's biggest companies—especially now in our post-pandemic world.

According to The CIO Outlook for 2021 from Constellation Research, "The CIO Survey 2020 data paints a fairly stark picture of the human situation due to COVID. Just under two-thirds of CIOs said that a top challenge of the pandemic was the mental, psychological, and physical well-being of workers."[89]

You bet the implications of employee health and happiness can be felt on the bottom line.

---

[89] Dion Hinchcliffe, "The CIO Outlook for 2021: Delivering Business ROI at Scale," Constellation Research, October 23, 2020, https://www.constellationr.com/research/cio-outlook-2021-delivering-business-roi-scale.

Take something as seemingly innocuous as a person's residence information. Many people don't realize how critical it is to an employer to have completeness and accuracy of this data. What difference does it make if my employer has up-to-date information on where I live? Well, for one thing, in the U.S., where a person lives is a key component that determines the payroll taxes on their paystub.

And if a person leaves their job, the employer has to give that person an accurate pay slip within 24 hours. But if the employer doesn't have the right residential information, they can't give the former employee an accurate number. And if they don't get that accurate number to the person within 24 hours or if it's inaccurate, the company faces a $6,000 fine.

Now let's say you're a retailer like Walmart or Walgreens with hundreds of thousands of employees (as I write this, Walmart has over 2 million employees worldwide[90] and Walgreens over 200,000[91]). Let's say Walmart has an employee attrition rate of 10 percent (for the sake of argument; I am not saying they do); that would be in excess of 20,000 people in any given year.

Of those, let's say just 20 percent of those people have inaccurate final paychecks because of errors in personal data. That's 4,000 X $6,000 = $24 million in potential fines. That's a considerable amount of change.

A DAP can be configured to reduce the potential for these types of gaps. When you really stop to think about it at a deeper level, what are these numbers trying to measure? Data accuracy? Process completion?

Or are they measuring people being happy? If the end goal is to get to happiness and if you have a high happiness index, it can be a real differentiator for the company; a real attraction for people to come work for you and stay with you.

If your company experiences first-day employee churn, you understand what I mean. If your organization operates in an environment where there are skills shortages, you get what I mean. Keeping talent today is tough. Attracting talent tomorrow will be harder.

---

90 "Company Facts," Walmart, accessed May 14, 2021, https://corporate.walmart.com/newsroom/company-facts.

91 "Facts and FAQs," Walgreens, accessed May 14, 2021, https://news.walgreens.com/fact-sheets/frequently-asked-questions.htm.

Here's another example showing how important it is to truly have a value framework in place. Let's say that there are parts of the program that are up and running. The good news is you're already crawling. But how do you begin to walk and run? Most organizations continue to crawl because they simply cannot pinpoint where they're having problems learning to walk. With a digital adoption platform in place, they now have the ability to baseline where there are.

A DAP allows management to dive into the baby user data. Pre-DAP, this was at best an educated guess. Now leaders can inspect and dissect the data. They can see the number of people using a particular technology and how long a user session lasts.

This means the leaders can make better purchasing decisions. "Why did we buy so many subscriptions to this software?" they might ask themselves. "We now know we only need half the number of subscriptions."

Right there they've halved their costs from a runtime cost perspective.

Or maybe they find that only 23 percent of their baby users are using a vital application. A DAP gives business leaders the ability to dive in and determine where the friction is and how much friction the business can accept. Only then can they determine and create intervention events in the process to smooth it out so usage goes up. Whatever the case may be (buy fewer subscriptions or increase usage), it all ties back to the value framework established at the beginning.

When value frameworks with the appropriate baselines are used correctly, not only can you measure and see how your baby users turn into superheroes, but also the benefits spread throughout the entire organization turning it into a superhero too.

Spoiler Alert: Don't be too surprised if you can't find much baseline data. Don't fret too much. Deploy the DAP, track a few events and let the data present the baseline. No need for expensive hypothesizing or consultants.

Three Layers of Superheroes

Ultimately, the hero in all this is the individual baby user. The baby user exists across the three layers we will describe; program, operational, and strategic level. The implications are simple—create superheroes at each level, and you create a superhero organization.

The Program Level Superheroes

These are the people on the ground. Typically, they are customer-facing or performing back-office functions that keep the engine of the organization turning. They are the frontline workers of every organization and are impacted the most by changes in processes or the rollout of new technology assets because they need to use the tools to complete their tasks.

In its simplest form, their business issue is that they are unable to meet or exceed their business objectives for the week, month, quarter, or year because they are challenged with their technology stack. The types of traditional costs that organizations face at this level of the challenge include system onboarding costs, increased support ticket costs, and travel and expense costs.

To emerge as superheroes, the program-level super-user would benefit immensely from a digital concierge that would remove those friction points allowing them to soar to greater heights through the ever-changing applications landscape, help them minimize data entry errors, and to complete business processes in shorter amounts of time allowing the focus to be on the customer.

The implications of failing here are that work simply cannot or doesn't get out of first gear and frustration begins to build at ground zero. If work doesn't get out of first gear, think about the amount of value lost simply because program-level users are chained, unable to break free to soar. Surely the focus on creating superheroes needs to here and with a DAP the reality of an individual personal digital concierge can be a reality.

The Operational Superhero

It is not uncommon for the operational user to be fixated on metrics and industry benchmarks. Sometimes operational managers focus on the numbers and not the means to improve the numbers. Throwing more resources at a problem is the typical solution to the problem. Most hyper-growth companies flood their sales teams with additional head count in search of additional revenue as opposed to thinking more strategically on how to drive increased share of wallet.

One is an easier yet higher-risk solution. If we shift our thoughts to delivering a service, like in a call center, then our focus is typically on metrics like average handling time (AHT). Drive that metric down and you are in a good place. Fail and you find yourself thinking about quicker time to productivity strategies for onboarding new reps.

Wouldn't it be great if we could build an infrastructure that not only allowed for faster onboarding but also drives down AHT? This is the core tenant of a DAP.

Managers can leverage the insights to further sharpen their grip of AHT by leveraging the insights to understand where friction exists for their baby superheroes, tweaking user journeys to a point akin to sharpening a superhero's power.

The implications of AHT heading in the wrong direction are like that snowball accelerating down the mountainside. With each revolution, the cost impact builds and multiplies exponentially. Organizations typically react only once they begin to experience the implications of not having these superheroes.

For the operational superhero, his role is to create as many program-level superheroes as possible. If he can help to reduce call handling times for one baby user that would be terrific but to be able to scale that across dozens, hundreds, and sometimes thousands of baby users would be amazing and have far-reaching P&L implications.

Roche, a global healthcare and biotechnology leader, found that it was near impossible to keep its people proficient with the myriad of software applications and updates they needed to do their jobs. In 2009, they rolled out a new enterprise-wide HR system.[92]

This required the creation of hundreds of e-learning materials in more than 10 languages. Think about the multiplier effect of having to build out support content traditionally ten times over and then have to maintain and update the content. Most organizations had invested in instructional designers but soon found converting rich storyboards into rich user experiences was a bridge too far.

At Roche, their plan included thousands of classroom training sessions around the world. Think about the coordination costs, never mind the travel, time, and expense costs of the exercise. Oh, and they also had to provide an on-demand help and support mechanism for their employees after the training event.

As Ralph Boer, head of Roche's IT learning solutions told Constellation Research, "The employee experience was terrible—they got stuck and were very frustrated."[93] Roche implemented a DAP to help resolve all the training hurdles that were keeping their large employee population from being productive and efficient.

The company found the DAP to be an effective solution. Training was reduced significantly (cost savings) and because users had in-application assistance, they were able to navigate effortlessly through the new digital without the need for traditional support. Employee satisfaction increased, which was reflected in their employee satisfaction ratings and confidence in using the application. Most significantly, the help desk remained silent, which meant support agents could be redeployed to more customer-facing activities.

The changes across the organization were so profound that they adopted a new operational mantra, "While people are working, they're learning and while people are learning, they're working."[94]

The Roche story is an example of how an organization can build an army of superheroes. The DAP unleashed the power of users allowing them

---

92   "Ralph Borer," Constellation Research, accessed May 19, 2021, https://www.constellationr.com/node/15785/vote/application/view/511.

93   Ibid.

94   Ibid.

to love work and be more productive.

For Ralph and Roche, their efforts were recognized in 2018 when they received the Constellation Research Supernova Award for Employee Experience. Today, they have their DAP deployed across 50-plus corporate applications globally.[95]

The Leadership Superheroes

This third level of superheroes is almost at the Justice League level. These are the C-suite folks who stand in front of boards and shareholders and report on the results of the corporate objectives that have been agreed at the start of the year.

Senior executives need to be predictable in their business results. Predictability breeds confidence and trust because it brings a degree of stability to the share price. It gives the executive the credit to be able to tweak the agenda when needed.

The insights from a DAP allow executives to de-risk their strategies. If the expectation is to tighten the corporate belt and reduce operating costs by 10 percent, a DAP allows the organization to think about how they leverage program-level users to perform multiple tasks.

In the past, this would not be possible but with a digital concierge courtesy of a DAP, organizations can begin to leverage superheroes with one superpower and onboard and support them to grow their powers. Today, with DAP, we begin to see the emergence of the multifaceted employee or what some consulting firms call the elastic workforce. In short, we are leveraging generalists and using a DAP to give them specialist powers. The simple answer of the past, throwing more heads at the problem, becomes a distant strategy.

Remember CHRISTUS Health—by helping their finance department and nursing staff get superpowers specific to including patient codes on bills, baby users began to run and soar to the tune of driving an additional $1 million to the bottom line each month.[96]

---

95   Ibid.

96   https://www.walkme.com/solutions/use-case/business-continuity/

DAPs are designed to drive business outcomes and they can. If you are smart, IT and procurement teams would use the insights from a DAP to keep vendors honest with licensing costs. All because of a DAP-centered transformation.

Let's look at this from another angle and through the eyes of a company that knows technology: IBM.

IBM offers a plethora of complex digital tools and support to companies going through digital transformations. This means that, by extension, any digital transformation obstacles experienced by those companies have a direct negative effect on IBM. Specifically, in the form of lower sales conversions, fewer repeat sales, and increased support costs.

IBM learned in significant and measurable terms that using a DAP to help onboard and train its B2B digital transformation customers helps streamline the onboarding process and leads to successful transformation.

"First and foremost, we were able to improve user adoption early on, resulting in 6X higher user retention and 4X better conversion rates from trials to subscriptions," says Nilanjan Adhya, IBM's chief digital officer. "We enabled faster onboarding of our products, but we also enabled them to get support right at the point in the product where they need it."[97]

You may ask why. Simply put, users or more importantly customers were happy. They found the technology easy to use. They used more of the functionality and got more value out of the software. It almost became second nature and subconsciously a barrier to exit formed. They had created superheroes in their customer base.

With its substantial increases in sales conversions (as high as 300 percent in early adopter conversions) and repeat sales, as well as significant reductions in support costs,[98] IBM is a powerful example that when you employ a DAP, you're creating superheroes from the ground up and it expands up and throughout your organization to create superheroes at even the highest levels.

Again, the question is, "Where do you want to end up?" Once you

---

97   "IBM Boosts Conversion Rate and Retention Rate with Digital Adoption Strategy and WalkMe," WalkMe, accessed May 19, 2021, https://www.walkme.com/customer-stories/ibm/.

98   Ibid.

know that, the key is then to build out user journeys and intervention events that help execute plans that permeate through the three levels that we have discussed.

Coming back to the Forrester report, a clear outcome that they found was that successful organizations (like Roche, IBM, Red Hat, CHRISTUS Health, et al.) that build proactive digital adoption strategies yield increasing value over time as high as 125 percent over a three-year horizon. Like any data-driven company, if leveraged correctly, it would make it difficult for similar types of companies to compete against this cohort.

The HERO Framework

The HERO Framework was designed by WalkMe, to help organizations measure the value they were getting from their DAP content.[99] Each letter represents a business objective tied to a range of performance indicators or business KPIs.

Happiness

In the digital adoption world, when we refer to happiness, we are really trying to understand from the end-user if they found the application easier to use or more helpful in the flow of their work given the presence of a DAP.

Users or customers at a program, process level typically don't get a say in the digital tool set that they need to use on a daily basis. The very same tool set that determines their ability to exceed their business objectives. It's akin to a professional tennis player not being able to pick her shoes, racket, string tension, and isotonic drink. It is like having one arm tied behind your back and being expected to beat Serena Williams.

For the purposes of baby users, it's actually very simple: The goal is for them to find the digital tools you give them helpful and easy to use. When and where they find a challenge or bump, they should either be given the

---

99 "Understanding the Value of Digital Adoption," Walk Me, accessed May 19, 2021, https://jay-marketplace.azureedge.net/app_resources/92/documentation/320_en.pdf.

opportunity to voice their displeasure or the analytics will shine a spotlight where work needs to be done. With a DAP, user happiness is easily measured through a range of strategies; a thumbs up or down at the end of a process, perhaps a range of emoji expressions to depict how you felt, or a more traditional net promoter scores, customer satisfaction scale ranking.

Delighted users do their best work when the system part of their day is frictionless, allowing them to focus on the customer and building out the value of that relationship.

Engagement

In the digital adoption world, engagement refers to whether users are using applications in a consistent manner. We look to see if they become more comfortable using the application set. The measurement is typically around process completion and how much of the underlying application is being used and how much of the DAP content is being engaged with.

Simply put, it's how quickly and thoroughly your baby users adopt applications, complete tasks, and come back to use the tools again. A DAP allows you to precisely measure these three metrics, measure where and why they might be falling short, and create content to smooth over these friction points.

For an organization, process completion is the most significant engagement metric. Users may start off crawling and give up. The significance of the DAP is that it creates a safe environment where baby users can't get lost, resulting in their confidence growing alongside their desire to hone those superpowers further.

Realization of Value

As the benefits of the DAP begin to take root, different business levers begin to be impacted in a positive manner. For example, with the digital concierge, L&D departments will see training savings in terms of class sessions and content curation. Support functions such as help desks become less popular because baby users are walking and running.

Where a DAP is used strategically in product development, development costs accelerate down due to the nature of the technology and the ability for product houses to iterate at pace and scale. Agile promised quarterly cycles. DAP could in theory reduce that to a matter of days. We saw how significant an impact a DAP had on the IBM products business.

Operational Excellence

This is essentially your organization being in a state of readiness to be able to execute on priorities as a normal course of business. Digital adoption content is curated with key indicators in mind such as *data validation* to ensure the right source data doesn't disrupt a downstream process like the correct bank account number format flowing downstream to enable payroll from being executed. When we talk about data validation, we usually think of ensuring information is correct for the sake of efficiency. Yet we often forget how costly poor data validation can be. Just ask Citibank and Revlon.

In August of 2020, a subcontractor for Citibank mixed up the boxes to check in a loan payment application. The subcontractor thought he was sending $7.8 million in interest payments to Revlon's creditors. In fact, due to the application's confusing user interface, the subcontractor accidentally sent $900 million, effectively paying off the principle of Revlon's debt much sooner than the company was prepared.[100]

Once Citibank recognized the mistake, the company scrambled to recoup the money from Revlon's creditors, managing to bring back $400 million. But many of Revlon's creditors claimed they had a legal right to keep the funds despite the money being sent in error.

As of this writing, Citi had lost "its bid to reclaim the cash from the $900 million mistake."[101]

Citibank was certain they had built-in operational controls to prevent such costly mistakes. For instance, the payments required three levels of

---

100 Elisa Martinuzzi, "Citi's $900 Million Loan Error Is Still Perplexing," Bloomberg, udated August 25, 2020, https://www.bloomberg.com/opinion/articles/2020-08-25/citigroup-s-900-million-revlon-loan-error-is-still-perplexing.

101 Cowley, Stacy. "Citi Loses Its Bid to Reclaim Cash from a $900 Million Mistake." The New York Times. The New York Times, February 16, 2021. https://www.nytimes.com/2021/02/16/business/citibank-revlon-loan.html.

approval before they could be made.

Yet the subcontractor, one of the subcontractor's supervisors, and an executive at Citibank all failed to catch the checkbox mistakes in the payment application. Had Citibank employed a DAP to validate its payment processes, ensuring the right boxes were checked and the correct dollar amounts were declared, Citibank and Revlon would have been able to avoid learning a $500 million lesson the hard way.

Leveraging change managers and instructional designers to translate storyboards to user experiences that cater to different digital IQs in the organization creating an on-demand help mechanism at any part of the flow of work.

Each user journey is curated with the baby user in mind with efficiency and time savings core to content design. When you do this, you're running optimally, efficiently, and elegantly. What's more, you're poised and ready to execute new key priorities.

But Wait, Here Comes a Big Twist!

Most organizations look at value realization in their own distinct silo. Instead of just focusing on Happiness or Operational Excellence in isolation, the secret here is to look for logical combinations, typically where the friction impacts the P&L. You can have it all if you think logically around the user journey; users being happy, processes being completed in lower time, data being accurate, avoiding compliance pitfalls whilst reducing support and training costs.

I will share with you an example of how an organization reimagined the first experience an employee had during onboarding. They realized that first impressions do matter and the data from their onboarding surveys reflected a less than stellar first experience.

New employees were required to update their banking information by the 21st of the month and they needed to order their own corporate mobile phones. Now without Marge, these "simple" tasks placed a burden on support business partners.

By leveraging the value framework, designing the user journey, and being clear on where the friction points were, the team built out an experience that launched a user from a welcome email into the personal information section. There, the banking information needed to be updated, so they automated all the empty clicks within the process, validating the format of the banking account number.

Then the DAP took the user cross-application to the procurement application, skipping screens to go directly to the mobile phone page, where the user selects his preferred device.

Now as each process is successfully completed, a thumbs up/down survey is presented with a scaled rating at the end.

By doing this, the team was able to measure process completion and time to completion, ensure data integrity, and measure happiness. They were also able to iterate, driving process improvements with the insights engine allowing new employees to feel like superheroes from their first day of work.

CHAPTER 8

CONTENT: THE ONCE AND FUTURE KING

When the COVID-19 pandemic first exploded onto the world stage in early 2020, the world knew very little about the virus. Few facts were available and the internet was flush with gossip, innuendo, and fear-mongering. Many organizations weren't quite sure how best to communicate with their employees about the virus.

Some employers found the task even more difficult because of the geographic spread of their people. Orica, the Australian explosives company, has people spread across more than 100 countries in some of the most remote parts of the earth.[102]

Given the nature of their industry, employee health and safety are big concerns for Orica. It was important for leadership that the employees remained connected with the changing situation associated with the growing pandemic. The traditional way of communicating was to push out emails, but Greg Woulfe, head of learning and development, saw the situation as an opportunity for the company to rethink how accurate information could be shared with employees.

Woulfe's immediate reaction that morning was to open his DAP editor

---

102 "Orica CEO: It's Critical to Keep Mining Exports Going," the *Australian*, April 3, 2020.

and log into his DAP store where he was able to search and find some pre-built content he could leverage. He added that to his already pre-built Orica branded template, added a link to the World Health Organization website where the latest factual information regarding the virus could be found. He then added an additional link to Orica's Employee Health and Safety SharePoint page, which outlined the company's guidance on the virus.

Within 10 minutes, a "pop-up" (or ShoutOut, in DAP lingo) appeared each time someone logged onto the company portal.

Ten minutes is all it took. Greg literally rolled out of bed, logged on to his computer, and published content that got pushed to employees looking for answers. Think about that for a moment.

There was a lot of uncertainty. Our daily lives were changing. We didn't know what tomorrow would look like. People needed specific, relevant, and accurate information. And within 10 minutes, Greg was able to provide just what the employees needed, right when they needed it and, more critically, in the location where most employees would be looking for the information.

Using a DAP that was designed with the everyday, functional user in mind afforded Greg the ability to create and push that message out to their 16,000 employees in a matter of minutes. More importantly, the company could track who had actually engaged with the message, who had gone to the WHO website, and who had gone to the internal portal.

In the process, Greg was able to reduce the chatter, the pressure on managers whose employees were looking for answers, and the help desk staff who now could quickly redirect employees to the exact location on the site where the relevant information could be found.

The Orica story highlights some key lessons in the digital world. When leveraged correctly, a DAP can help you pivot a whole business process even under the direst of circumstances.

Remember the Australian bushfires in Chapter 1? If you remember, the insurance company used a DAP to revamp their claims process in a matter of weeks to remove the bottlenecks that were backing up claims and delaying much-needed help for their policyholders.

They were able to react quickly because they had a formal structure around their DAP content curation process. They were able to create and revise DAP content as needed to address friction points as they arose. By keeping their DAP content creation in-house and in the hands of the people on the frontlines closest to the processes, they were able to pivot at a pace that's almost inconceivable for most large corporate institutions.

Content is and will always be king. It is what draws people to a medium or platform. Clichés are clichés for a reason: They work. They do the trick. They are rooted in truth. This is no truer than with a DAP, but the content must first be relevant to the user and it must be actionable.

Yet, I'm amazed at how often organizations are caught by surprise when they realize that they actually need to invest in and build content. It is almost like an "aha" moment that's some version of, "Oh wait, I have to create DAP content too? I have more work to do!"

Spoiler alert, yes, you have to create content for your DAP. It is content that fuels the transformation of your crawling baby users into flying superheroes adept at using the digital tools you give them. It is the content that, if designed for the flow of work, will take out current and future downstream costs.

Another word of advice: If you decide to outsource the content build process in its entirety, you run the risk of missing out on critical learnings about how your organization needs to evolve into new ways of working. You need the experience of creating DAP content to truly understand what digital transformation truly means to your organization.

In the recent *Harvard Business Review* Analytics Report on "The State of Digital Adoption 2021," the authors write that making the most of technology is a job that many companies (73 percent) assign to their own people while only 5 percent rely on the original software developer. Just 8 percent turn to global systems integrators or other consultants.[103] I see these figures shifting around a little in the short to medium term as companies dabble and gain experience with DAPs.

---

103 "The State of Digital Adoption 2021," *Harvard Business Review*, April 1, 2021, https://hbr.org/
   sponsored/2021/04/the-state-of-digital-adoption-2021.

There are many reasons for this; most notably that driving adoption is an intimate organizational process. In-house teams have the intimate organizational understanding and context necessary when it comes to people, processes, and technology that third-party teams lack by default.

As an aside, my experience tells me there *can* be a healthy middle ground when it comes to blending an internal-external team to create content. When I look at DAP programs, I look at things in three levels:

1. Content curation
2. Insights as a service
3. Operating models in new ways of working

There are models in which each of these functions can be done internally or externally or a combination of the two. When domain expertise is blended with company context, that's when the magic can happen, so to speak. It comes down to the team—internal, external, or blended—having the skills, experience, and domain expertise.

The truth of the matter is that when you first unwrap your DAP, it pretty much comes with a set of instructions on how to build content and directions to the storefront where a bunch of prebuilt templates may reside.

To drive value from the DAP, you will need to build content that is specific to your organization. There will be some DAPs that will include application-specific templates and generic content templates. These will get you up and running quickly but don't expect any DAP platform to simply plug-and-play into your specific world. The key is to look for quick wins and not to try to solve for world peace.

As an example, on April 3, 2020, Singapore's Prime Minister, Lee Hsien Loong, announced the start of an attempt to manage the spread of the COVID-19 virus there. Schools were closed and home learning would be in effect, an order that would stay in place for two months.[104]

During that time schools, teachers scrambled to build out content for home-based learning. Parents, too, scrambled because everything was cen-

---

104 Lee Hsien Loong, "PM Lee on the COVID-19 Situation in Singapore on 3 April 2020," Facebook video, April 3, 2020, https://fb.watch/5B73KEI0gF/.

tered around the Student Learning System, which many of us didn't know how to access, never mind use.

To train to use their digital tools for this new way of teaching, teachers were guided through their lesson planning and execution with the assistance of a DAP. But the country didn't stop there. The DAP-driven teaching transformation wasn't only efficient and effective for helping teachers, but it also proved easy and effective for bringing along students and parents to this new way of learning too.

Fast-forward one year, today both teachers and students are leveraging a DAP to ensure the focus is on the content and not the journey to access the content.[105] All across the country tens of thousands of parents were breathing huge sighs of relief and, in the process, putting a smile on many Singaporean's faces.

The challenge remains that as a collective, organizations did not embrace cloud 1.0 as an opportunity to leverage standard out-of-the-box business processes. The general lack of desire to simplify and standardize has meant a missed opportunity in general terms. Templates, while an attractive proposition, continue to be a nice idea as opposed to a standard reality. Any templates that a DAP provides will still provide benefits in that they will serve as a launchpad for users to get off the ground and running faster. They may need to be tweaked around the edges, but it is at least a start to accelerate that business value realization process.

In an ideal world, technology would be deployed as standard out of the box, but we live in a world where we still can't agree on basic terminology. Is it a "goal" or "objective" setting process? People actually debate this, even if it is the same process. Yup, we can't agree on terminology so what hope is there to agree on the same steps in basic process flows? So instead of focusing on what we can't change, we need to focus on the art of the possible. Content needs to be owned by people who understand the direction in which you want to head.

Now that we have established that standardization and change are going

105   Tan Seng Chee and Tsering Wangyal, "Here's How Technology Can Transform Learning and Education," *Today*, March 23, 2021, https://www.todayonline.com/commentary/heres-how-technology-can-transform-learning-and-education.

to be difficult (almost impossible) because in all transformations we are actually focusing on new ways of working, we must focus on how to get users crawling, walking, and running. As an organization, you go out and hire the best available talent. You follow that up with building either the best product you can or the best service offering in the market, and yet somehow you fail to get the business results you had hoped for.

It's like having the best Formula One car and the best pit crew and driver but when you hit the ignition, the engine doesn't start. Why? Because there was no fuel in the tank. The DAP content is the fuel. It not only allows you to get out of the pit but helps you glide through the gears, helping the driver understand when to brake, when to accelerate, when to come in for a tire change and get back out in under 16 seconds, finishing on the podium each and every time. This is how baby users accelerate through the gears from crawling, walking, and finally running.

Most companies leave this missing ingredient out of their digital transformation programs. Like a car that needs fuel each time it attempts to complete a lap, most users will need help not just during the hyper-care stage of the technology implementation but through the user journey. Most organizations see success being the go-live event and continue to support the program through a three-month process post–go-live called "hyper-care." They leave just about enough gas in the tank to get to this milestone in the program, often giving little if not any consideration to what happens after the event.

The organizations that see the value of DAP realize the value of content over time and will invest in a strategy for building content. Throughout this chapter, I will endeavor to unpack the thought process about content creation.

The starting point must always be the business issue you are trying to impact positively. The challenge is to think about how to accommodate each element of potential friction in the user journey.

The content should be designed in such a way that it can be triggered by a user at any point of the journey. Built once to accommodate many different scenarios as opposed to building content many times for many different user types. While this sounds like a "one-size-fits-all" scenario it actually is "all-scenarios-in-one." This is an important first step because creating DAP content for the sake of building content will set you up for expensive failure.

For a DAP to be impactful in your digital transformation program, it is important to keep the following in mind:

1. Think about what content users will need and when they will need it. Don't boil the ocean. It's not about the volume of content. If you are a new salesperson, you probably will need content to help you build out your territory as opposed to how to book a deal. It's about having the right content, presented to the appropriate user at the right time so that your baby users can be superheroes.

2. The content you build must be built with a value framework in mind to impact the business. Do you have some key metrics that are tied to your original business case? If so, build to solve for that. You can build content that not only helps to drive process completion but does so with speed and accuracy in mind that you can measure. Content that cannot be tied back to a measurement is merely layering additional cost and friction to the business.

3. Organizations must be able to build content in an agile and quick manner. A DAP is designed to help a business pivot. The limitations are based on internal capability. A DAP must be easy to use. A non-technical person should be able to build DAP content. You must place the power in the hands of the everyday user. You and I should know the basics. A process owner should be able to build what they need without a coding background and there should be GPS-like help in building the content curation tool.

4. Machine learning algorithms must be baked into any DAP platform so that the platform can learn from errors and user mistakes. While no algorithm is perfect, it must improve with data sets, be-

coming more robust each time there is a new intervention event.

5. Given the volume of content that will be created, a DAP must have some form of automated testing capabilities running in the background, learning from breaks in content and alerting the user to where fixes need to be applied.

Right Content, Right Time

It seems obvious that creating a bunch of content for the sake of having a bunch of content won't move the needle in your digital transformation program. Often, in a rush of excitement and enthusiasm, organizations rush out to create a bucket load of content because they believe, wrongly, that some content is good but more content is better.

But it's not about the volume of content. It's about how strategic your DAP content is. It's about building content that will impact your business objectives by accelerating your baby user's evolution into superhero status. It's about how we get them to use the company's digital tools and processes effortlessly and in a consistent manner. It is the content that creates the superhero. But the right impactful content can also help unlock cashable benefits that fuel the strategic objectives of the company.

Again, it's not about tossing up just any old content. When you provide the right DAP content (relevant to the user, easy to follow, tied to business goals) at the right time (that exact moment when your baby users need that specific bit of help from the DAP), your DAP will play a critical part in helping your baby users to soar.

Remember, people forget. Never lose sight of the significance of the forgetting curve. People will leave the organization, change roles within the organization, and new baby users will arrive. So, you must have a content strategy. Thinking about it strategically will not only ensure that the content will remain relevant in the years to come but will act as a platform for accelerated change in the new ways of working which are the underlying foundations of the transformation program.

Your Own Content Factory

Inevitably, soon after having that "aha" moment about the need to create DAP content, you will need to start thinking about who will be accountable for the content, how many content builders you will need, where you should look for these talents, and where they need to be placed strategically.

Someone will suggest outsourcing the content work. There will be a strong temptation to bring in user experience designers, graphic designers, content creators, and outside subject matter experts to craft and polish DAP content.

Don't be tempted to concede ownership too early in the process. At the simplest level, digital transformation programs are about new ways of working. If you outsource the opportunity to understand how your users are reacting to these new ways of working, you will never get a handle on the friction or collision points.

In the short term, it is critical to leverage expertise to learn and harness the power of a DAP. To do that you should start with a hybrid approach where you leverage the technical product expertise of your DAP provider and blend it with the functional, business process knowledge of your team. An initial professional services engagement should include a very clear enablement plan for your resources and an agreed co-build strategy with the DAP provider always doing the quality assurance of any content built. Most of the organizations I work with think about the content build in three phases.

In phase one, the product principle builds the vast majority of the content while the customer builds about 20 percent with all the QA being done by the product principle. In phase two, the customer carries the weight of the build, perhaps 80 percent to 20 percent with the product principle owning the minority of the builds but still owning the QA. The third phase sees the customer owning all of the build given the improved proficiency in the content curation but with the product principle owning the QA.

This simple plan is actually quite critical because in the short term it allows you the ability to leverage technical expertise to learn and formulate a mid-and long-term strategy. As your team matures, you will be best placed to think about what fits your organization best. Should you outsource content build? Should you keep the management of the analytics in-house? Should you just keep process design in-house and outsource the rest of the value chain?

There isn't a one-size-fits-all model but what is clear, for a DAP strategy to be successful, you will need the internal capability, and depending on the depth of that capability, you can then make the right determinations.

Don't shortchange your organization's success by shifting the responsibility of content build to a third party exclusively. This short-lived advantage of a lighter workload will come back to haunt you in the medium term. There will be vendors who will tempt you with "free" services and will encourage you to let them build all your DAP content for you. By doing this, you are inadvertently building out a crutch that you will be forced to lean on; one that hinders your organization's ability to react in an ever-changing business landscape.

A DAP strategy will drive new ways of working within your organization. For it to have the desired impact, your organization will need to flex and accommodate a different type of resource being embedded within a program, department, or even across the organization. But outsourcing the content curation process exclusively will hinder the cultural shift of allowing the DAP integration into the tissue of your organization's new ways of working.

It may sound like I am pro-internal or anti-external involvement. This is not the case. The decisions you make should take into account where the skills sit. In many cases, the experience will sit externally but this external expertise must be blended with internal context for success to be had.

Where you start depends on where you sit on the maturity continuum of DAP implementations. Is this your first foray into the DAP world or have you earned your stripes from a few initial deployments?

If you are at the exploration phase and you are using a DAP to help solve isolated pains across an application, then look to leverage someone within your organization to make the DAP platform part of his or her world. I recommend looking for two if not three resources who would add DAP builder skills to their repertoire. During this phase, it is important to leverage the vendor's capabilities and capacity because this is the heart of Superhero University.

Now as the benefits get realized and the demand for more superheroes grows, the question will come. Do we continue to build or do we buy the competence? Well, again, it depends. Remember to always keep the following question in mind, "Are we solving friction around tech dependencies that are impacting our corporate strategic objectives?"

When we look at content curation, it isn't merely about building the content. It is about understanding the problem. It is about understanding the journey and possible start-stop points. It is about being able to leverage the insights and making a judgment call on what content needs to be prioritized. As these decisions become more relevant so will the biggest question of them all.

Do we change the organization structure to support this new way of working? Or do we outsource the end-to-end process? The question that will confront organizations will be, "Do we keep it all in-house, outsource the entire process or just farm out the plumbing?" It all comes down to whether the DAP content is helping solve a basic program challenge or a core business issue that can be defined, quantified, and is time-bound.

Ask yourself this question: "How much of your core competence do you currently outsource?" If you are a product company, do you outsource product development? If you are a sales-driven organization, would you consider outsourcing the sales function to a third party? I think the answer is plain and obvious.

The big shift will come as you evolve from a siloed, single application problem-solving dimension to one where the DAP maturity extends across the organization and is embedded in your strategic business issues.

There are benefits to keeping all the work in-house in the initial stages. It will force you to understand the value proposition of the DAP. There are countless examples where a customer has said to me, "Oh, I didn't know you could measure employee satisfaction through a survey or you really can build a cross-application process."

Keep the platform in-house. Assign resources to play with the platform. Build-out content. Learn, use the analytics and tweak the content. Each tweak brings more learning and, in turn, more small wins

By creating your own mini-DAP content factory, you will learn first-hand about the true value of the platform (not tool, not application, but platform). This understanding will allow you to level set on the type of skills you will need as demand for DAP content accelerates. It will also help you determine what you own, what you outsource, and why.

The next big question is where will you find the people with the organizational and process knowledge to ensure your content is strategic and relevant? It turns out that there are three logical breeding grounds for this type of resource.

The first is the functional user, i.e., the person who built the process (superhero user or subject matter expert). The second is the process user, i.e., the person confronted by the process each day as he or she uses the digital tool. The third is the support center agent who has the challenge of helping to resolve these challenges daily from baby users.

Think about it, if you are trying to take the friction out of the sales technology stack, who better to ask than the salesperson himself? After all, he or she is going to know what sales support content he or she needs.

The people on the front lines are going to be your best guides to creating highly relevant content that addresses your most pressing needs. Not only are these frontline colleagues your best subject matter experts, but they're also the baby users who'll first use the DAP to become the inaugural graduating class of your organization's Superhero University.

The other gold mine for DAP content curators sits in your support centers. Who better than your support specialist to tell you which processes they see as the biggest (most repeat) offending processes contributing to increased call volumes and average handling times?

Your in-house content factory is your Superhero University.

I can almost hear you saying, "Raj, it's all well and good that my frontline colleagues will help create our first batch of DAP content in your content factory, but how do we get that knowledge out of their heads? And who takes that knowledge and builds it out as our DAP content? Who tests it and revises it as needed?"

In other words, "Who will do the actual, hands-on work of creating the content?"

The answer: those same frontline colleagues.

If you choose your DAP wisely, it should be easy to use. There should be content that helps the user build the content. Anyone should be able to build content or at least understand the functional elements that a DAP provides. As a rule of thumb, my counsel to customers about content curation has always been as follows:

1. Are you solving a quantifiable business problem?
2. Does the solution mitigate a resource (Marge leaving) or operational risk?
3. Do the analytics support the need to build content? If so, refer to numbers 1.
4. Does the DAP provider have benchmark data where other organizations have struggled? Why reinvent the wheel? Leverage the experience.
5. Does the DAP provide a range of templates?
6. Can we follow a process calendar that will allow us to prioritize content based on when it will actually be needed?

Eventually, there may come a time when your DAP content scales to a point where the mini-DAP factory needs to make some critical decisions. For content to be relevant, it needs to solve problems that are time-sensitive ("I need to get it done now") to the user on the frontlines. And the content needs to be built "at pace" to reduce the friction from the business.

There are two schools of thought.

1. Centralize the resources in a Center of Excellence of sorts, or
2. Push the content curation deeper into the business that's closer

to the customer.

As the Forrester study clearly found, the value of a DAP snowballs with time, so the key is to think about how you are going to respond at a moment's notice.[106]

I am sure many of us have been involved in strategic planning. The challenge ultimately is how we respond to executing those plans. Typically, these plans get approved after the fact and we spend the rest of the year trying to catch up and execute on the expectations.

Immediately, managers feel they are behind the eight ball because they simply do not have the agility to scale resources that will drive the tech-dependent aspects of the strategy. Think of moving into a new market or launching a new product. How can we reduce the time to system competency of our resources?

A centralized center of excellence is a great concept but as your experience with the DAP matures you will begin to understand the strategic importance of different elements of the platform. I am sure you will realize the benefits of having core resources in-house, quite possibly residing in-country if not within a department.

The DAP builder will be a core team member just as the business analyst is today. My sense is that you will be able to start thinking more strategically about content. Will you need all the content on day one? Probably not. If you don't, given the lead time, wouldn't it make sense to outsource that to a lower-cost provider? It is plumbing after all.

Now to get to the plumbing, the insights derived from the DAP should drive what content should be built. This part of the process should be kept in-house at all costs, but this means you will need to upskill your internal resources to be more analytical in nature to help assess what friction points need to be resolved. Where will we have the biggest impact if we can take the friction out of the process?

If getting 10,000 people through a performance review process three months from now is something of strategic value like it was for Standard

---

106   WalkMe, "Forrester Analysis Found a Three-Year 368% ROI with WalkMe," accessed June 8, 2021, https://www.walkme.com/pages/forrester-tei-study/?t=19&eco=TEI&camp=TEI&abt1=7014G000001GN5J.

Chartered, then perhaps spending a bit of time building out the possible journey, pit stops, potholes, and then having them built in the offshore factory could be the right thing.

But if you are like Schneider Electric, no outsourced provider would notice, let alone care, if a process that took 22 seconds to complete was being used over 60,000 times over a month.[107] An internal analyst or DAP builder in the Quota Specialist Department may realize that any improvement would have a material impact on the business given the volume of usage. By leveraging DAP functionalities and automation, Schneider Electric was able to reduce that process down to just over *seven* seconds.

Sixty thousand times. What would the impact be if we could use a DAP and automate parts of the process? What type of impact could we have? Well, their internal resource got to work and was able to slice a full 15 seconds off the process:

60,000 processes completions X 15 seconds faster = 250 hours saved in that month

250 hours X $20/hour = $5,000/month on a single process

Given that these are quotation specialists, this rethink of the process did impact the volume and accuracy of quotes being pushed out to customers impacting sales in the process. It allowed the Schneider Electric team to accelerate quote delivery, resulting in a higher hit rate and more jobs won.

The question ultimately is who would have picked up this friction point? My view is that a core business must remain a core business and the insights-driven part of DAP must be kept in-house as a core competence. More than anything, you need your DAP content to be the right content. By "right," I mean it's strategic to your business and relevant to your baby users.

Not All DAP Content Creation Tools Are Created Equal

As the DAP landscape evolves, there will be a range of DAP providers. At last count, there were over 35 different options. The category has quickly evolved to be almost like Baskin Robbins' 31 flavors. The key to choosing the best option for you is understanding the problem you are trying to solve. Many people confuse in-application guidance as a DAP. That is a simple functional layer. As are engagement and automation. Going cross-application is a given. Here's what will set providers apart:

1. Does the provider have an insights-led mindset where content curation decisions are made based on data?

2. Can you understand how your baby users are using the technology one process step at a time?

3. How much experience does the DAP provider have?

4. Do they have a co-innovation program with customers and product owners?

The cloud, standardization, and the path to value realization will lead to the evolution and explosion of ecosystems and networks. Organizations that take advantage of this to collaborate, and even cooperate, will win. To accelerate value realization at a system level, like-minded organizations should come together and collaborate and co-innovate with their DAP provider around pre-built content. Tasks such as, "How I set a goal in my HR system?" or "How can I create an opportunity in my CRM?" can't be that different between organizations.

Today, HR service providers like Rizing are helping to build out standardized templates of common business processes. The nomenclature may be different but the system steps are the same. The blended Rizing and WalkMe team meets quarterly to decide what the insights are telling us, i.e., what processes are HR systems users are struggling with and what HR processes are around the corner given the HR process calendar. We agree on critical processes and that journey begins.

Several weekly meetings later, a bunch of standardized SAP SuccessFactors content is loaded into the template gallery free for all its customers to use. This type of forward thinking and a culture of paying it forward is helping companies realize the value in their DAPs much sooner than anticipated.

If we can remove whatever basic friction points the insights tell us exist, we start to accelerate value realization. Remember: Small wins are important, and critical to success. Always small wins. Think about it in terms of gaining yards to the first down in the NFL. Each yard is critical and can make the difference in winning and losing. When considering a DAP, you should demand this level of insight and DAP value acceleration. I can almost see a group of like-minded organizations creating a network of demanding more from the platforms and functional knowledge from DAP providers, challenging them to accelerate the content template build for the benefit of the entire network.

Technology category kings like Salesforce and Microsoft are kings not merely because of technology supremacy but because of what is "baked" into their technology. There is no shortcut to experience. You can build out functionality; two platforms can look the same, but the ultimate value between them can be vast.

Why? Experience. Experience brings a different type of knowledge.

It allows the DAP provider to embed into their solution all the lessons and expectations a user looks for but, more critically, needs. If you know that the robustness of your content weakens as steps are built or as you go cross application, that experience tells you to focus on strengthening the weaker content or working with a DAP provider with stronger machine-learning algorithms. You invest in algorithms that learn, beginning to understand the context of the content, and each time something breaks, it learns, gets smarter, and by default lowers the cost of maintaining content.

If I know there are different types of users of a process because the analytics are showing me abandonment spots or access points, etc., then I know what to build, where to build it, and how to engage a user.

The premium you pay incorporates the scars of others so that you avoid the same. A clear sign of product commitment and depth of R&D is the number of patents the DAP owns or has lodged. This gives you a feel for the DNA of the company and its desire to continuously innovate. Look on Google patents. Search and determine for yourself. Not all platforms are equal.

Here is another real-life example: When COVID-19 hit, many of us (organizations) had to pivot to work from home. For employers, it became critical to have completeness of employee data. From a risk perspective, companies needed to have emergency contact information and next of kin details. Now by sending out an email, we may get 20 percent completion rates. The challenge is how to engage with users to raise those completion levels.

One simple option would be to send an email with a link that, when clicked, takes the user into the application and guides, automates, and validates the data entry process. That alone may raise the completion rates by a further 20 percent. It may be time to get more blatant. We could build a pop-up on the screen of your laptop urging you to click on the same link. This may raise the completion by a further 30 percent.

We may give it another try and send the same message but this time only to people who haven't clicked the link. How do we know who hasn't? Simple, the insights from the DAP.

Sometimes the best way to find out the best solution is to ask different users.

For instance, in working with DAPs, my team and I have learned some users have grown accustomed to using a knowledge base to research the process before trying to execute it. That experience taught us we could place a button on that knowledge base article that, when clicked, took the user to the relevant system process, guiding, automating, and validating the data.

Experience. Nothing beats it.

The strength of a superhero comes down to the strength of their superpowers and what they have in their utility belts. Experience helps us to understand the add-ons required to improve these utility belts. It comes down to the context of the problem that you are trying to solve, not the functionality of the platform.

Now, I would like to make one thing clear. It may sound like I am discouraging the use of third-party services firms within your DAP strategy. To be crystal clear, this is not the case.

The role of external domain expertise is critical and should not be underestimated. The transformational impact of a DAP includes three tiers of value where third-party advisory firms (e.g. McKinsey & Company, Bain & Company, etc.), global system integrators (e.g. Accenture, Deloitte, PWC, etc.), and boutique services firms (e.g GuideMe, Charlton House) play critical roles in an organization's DAP Strategy.

Tier 1 of value comes from your content build. Once your internal capability matures and the volume of content grows, you should consider outsourcing this function for your non-core content build. Keep the QA process in-house or leverage your DAP provider's services team. You will always need internal capability in case you need to pivot or build something on the fly just like the Orica example that I shared earlier.

Tier 2 is what I like to call 'Insights-as-a-Service.' Your DAP platform will collate, aggregate, and present data points and insights. These will require interpretation and action. Many organizations appreciate the value of data but simply do not have the internal capability to interpret and make recommendations to drive more cashable benefits. A managed service from a third-party consulting firm would be a logical option where recommendations from a neutral party on a monthly or quarterly basis may prove invaluable.

But Tier 3 is where I believe organizations most need to leverage advisory firms. DAPs open up an opportunity for new ways of working. These new ways of working will need domain expertise to provide options on potential changes in operating models. Changes in organization design are not a one-size-fits-all model and your DAP strategy will need a shift in your current operating model if your organization is to evolve and scale. Domain expertise from both internal and external experts will be critical to the success of the transformation.

DAP Dos

Have you thought of your content as an asset?

Do you know how much content you are currently investing in to support your customers and employees through their technology relationship with you?

I typically start at the FAQ section on a website. How often are you updating this content? Do you know if the content is being used? Do you know if there are gaps in what the content is trying to solve? What is the cost of managing and updating content? What if I could tell you what content wasn't being used and as a result wasn't worth updating?

With a DAP this is available at a click of a button.

CHAPTER 9

TRANSFORMING YOUR TRANSFORMATION

Transforming your transformation seems like an oxymoron, but it is a real thing. Most digital transformations start out as something revolutionary that is designed to protect the organization from the challenges presented by those pesky disruptors. The tens if not hundreds of millions of dollars that are set aside and spent are done so with a singular view; protecting the organization from attack and in the process making the organization more relevant to the customer by making it easier for the customer to do business with it.

COVID-19 put a spotlight on how and where technology has played a key role in our lives. We now can acknowledge that many organizations can thrive in a remote world. We may not like the remote world, but we can thrive in it. What it means is that whilst businesses will always draw to a degree from their local workforce, we can hire from anywhere in the world. We don't need to worry about relocation. Gone are the days where we need to worry about visa quotas or whether we have enough seats in the office to accommodate our growth.

The events of 2020 have brought awareness about the need for organizations to shift their mindset when it comes to their employees. To date, we have talked about culture and people and the skills needed in the to-be world post-digital transformation. But now there is a very real shift in expectations.

In its simplest form, employees need to have the basics to get their work done, but their expectations are shifting. In an already troubled world, the basic expectation is that work needs to be easy to execute. If the employee cannot have a delightful experience in how they get work done, then they simply are not going to be the best version of themselves in their role. They won't be the most effective. Some may get frustrated, and possibly leave. That attrition will drive up the cost to hire and serve.

This has added yet another facet to your digital transformation program. You will need to think about the employee in different terms because their reality has changed. Their personal priorities have changed. If you don't believe me, just Google "pet ownership in times of COVID" or "baking in times of COVID." My personal favorite must be "chess in the times of COVID" where we have seen the impact of the Netflix series *The Queen's Gambit*. What you find are clear, data-driven positions on how personal priorities have shifted.

People have reprioritized fitness, diet, travel, etc., and organizations need to accommodate for this shift in mindset in their organizations' transformation programs. Work, in the eyes of the employee, has shifted quite dramatically for many, and organizations need to incorporate this shift. Work needs to become simplified. It's not unreasonable to assume cultural momentum will carry much of the current pandemic-driven reprioritization into our post-COVID world.

Pre-COVID, my work travel schedule (as much as I crave it again) used to be Sunday to Wednesday, three weeks a month. I am convinced that in the years to come my new normal, thanks to these new ways of working, will mean that my old reality is a distant memory. The pandemic has forced innovation to accelerate at a rate of knots. IT departments have been forced to rethink how to enable technologies to be more accessible from home. Not only have my options grown but my attitudes and desires have also evolved. I doubt I will be traveling at that same rate regardless of countries eventually opening up. This shift has allowed different friction points to bubble up.

Organizations have been so vested in their transformation plans that this fixed mentality blinded them from the need to continue to iterate, innovate, and be obsessed with the customer (in this case the customer is the employee). By standing still and not looking up while the world is moving forward many organizations have taken two, three, or four steps back. To avoid backward momentum, you need to keep baking disruptive ideas into your digital transformation program.

As a rule of thumb, I find that each of the following should be considered in the context of reducing the risk of poor execution in a digital transformation program:

1. Are there different ways we can make user adoption easier?
2. Is this alternative reliable and will it allow us more flexibility and agility?
3. Will it enhance the security and privacy of our employees and customers?
4. Is it a source of innovation and can we measure it?
5. Will it differentiate our proposition (e.g., Would you buy my coffee?)?

By rethinking these things, you begin to transform your original transformation, maybe not the plan but certainly the execution and value realization of it. But ignore this and all you're doing is kicking critical actions down the road. You have new root causes emerging and by deflecting, you are merely postponing things.

The stakes are high. In many cases, these transformations are a matter of survival. Failure could lead to extinction. Think Nokia. Think Blockbuster.

There is a plausible trend that suggests each time there has been a major disruption addressing fundamental friction points, customers gain a huge experiential and, in some cases, financial benefit while the disruptors see hyper-growth. Inevitably this leads to incumbents falling away.

Point 2 above should not be underplayed. Time-to-value is a real consideration. Transformation programs seem to take a lifetime. Even small changes seem to take a season or two. But with a DAP, you can drive incremental change in days.

The shortest implementation I have been part of was six days. The goal is to be able to impact the business in incremental bite sizes so that you begin to release the pressure valve. Small wins, quick wins. All too often the benefits of digital transformations are lagging indicators that are only visible quarters, years, even decades down the road. The reality is that time is not on your (CEO's) side.

The focus to date has been on how to WOW the customer. The shift now needs to be how to WOW the employee. Luckily, getting to the WOW will not require tons of inspiration or multiple moments of pure genius. But all organizations can change the trajectory of their digital transformation programs simply by shifting how they operate and engage their users.

We have discussed in detail how a DAP can quickly turn baby users into superhero users who rise to the occasion and help impact the transformation of your business. It is this superpower, to be an incubator of superheroes, that presents the opportunity. Digital transformations include as a core premise the notion of new ways of working. Simply put, organizations realize that to transform, both the customer and employee experience will need to change. Hence, new ways of working.

Anything short of these concrete changes in organizational mindset and execution is nothing more than that old definition of insanity: Doing the same thing you always did but expecting different results.

To start this revolution, many organizations have leveraged ideas like design thinking or shifting from Waterfall to Agile, whilst others have attempted to start with a fresh sheet of paper. Lemonade, the insurer, hit one million customers in four-and-a-half years in an industry where it took traditional players such as State Farm (22 years), Geico (28 years), and USAA (47 years) respectively.[108] They are selling insurance like those other companies, so what makes them different?

First, Lemonade needed to understand the customer and the internal employee. The insurance industry isn't an industry filled with trust. Customers don't see it as a must-have but as a necessary evil. The customer is filled with caution because the traditional experience has been adversarial rather than a safe Care Bear.

To counter this, Lemonade looked for the friction points in the process and basically disrupted an old industry. There is no paper in what was a paper-dependent process. There are no long, convoluted broker conversations, merely a playful chat with a bot that can take 90 seconds. This could never happen in the traditional process.

Everything about their success is about putting the consumer and their employee in the center. Not the technology, not the underwriter, and not the regulator. And the result is a service and product that consumers love and employees love to represent. They tell their friends. This advocacy drives more sales and data, which allows the product to be priced better. The savings can then be passed on to the consumer (sometimes 50 percent more than incumbents). Customers can and have adopted. Revenues are the clear measurement.

When we think about the customer experience, we think about how long it has typically taken to get a claim paid. Remember the family affected by the bushfires in Australia? Well, for Lemonade, in some cases claims were paid in three seconds! All the policyholder needed to do was open the application, pull their policy, and explain what happened. Use their mobile phone, make a recording and they were done. It is about delighting customers. They put the customer in the center of everything they do.

Putting it all together, you get something special. How special? A stock price that is five times the IPO price in the first six months of trading and a war chest of $1 billion in the bank.

---

108 "Lemonade Ends 2020 With over One Million Active Customers." Business Wire, December 31, 2020, https://www.businesswire.com/news/home/20201231005145/en/Lemonade-Ends-2020-With-Over-One-Million-Active-Customers.

Now, as much as many of you would like to be a Tesla or a Lemonade, the reality is the legacy foundations of your business simply won't allow for that level of a revolution. But it doesn't mean that you can't get to Apple- and Tesla-like net promoter scores or customer satisfaction scores. In fact, you've probably already done the heavy lifting of shifting from analog to digital. The rest of the transformation all lies in this notion of "new ways of working."

Your New Way of Working

Here's the basic premise: We need both the customer and employee to have a different, more elegant, simpler way of getting outcomes with your brand, product, or organization. The need to be delighted and be able to quantify the value of the experience, service, or product.

To understand the customer and employee more intimately, you, like Lemonade, Tesla, and Netflix, need data. The good news is your data is readily available. Deploy the DAP and simply let the data build.

Always remember: your data is the first step in transforming your trans- formation.

The second step is accepting that new ways of working will require some different skill sets. Note I said some, not the majority. More about these resources later on.

Also, we have discussed the need to treat content as an asset. This con- tent is what incubates your people from baby users to superheroes. As your content grows richer it not only accelerates the growth of your baby users into superhero status, but you begin to see the broader opportunity of cul- tivating a new type of superhero—the multifaceted employee.

The multifaceted employee is one who traditionally is considered a spe- cialist in his or her field. In the past, trying to teach an "old dog new tricks" has been an extremely costly exercise. But if we could bend the curve a little to create an environment where these specialists in one domain can add another domain to their kit bag, we could have a game-changing impact on a business.

Even if we merely get these people to walking status in the new specialization, it is a huge outcome. It allows organizations the ability to pivot with shifts in strategic objectives. Remember the insurance company? They leveraged generalists, using a DAP to incubate them to become superheroes who got up to jogging status in a matter of days.

Again, I can't say this too many times or any more bluntly than this: The only way to arrive at this is to truly rethink your content strategy.

We've all heard of Software as a Service (SaaS) or Platform as a Service (PaaS). Why not try to evolve to Content as a Service (CaaS)?

This shift in mindset will afford an organization the flexibility and visibility to understand what content is required, by whom and when. But it requires an internal capability to understand how to leverage a DAP, both the data it provides and the content driven by that data.

It does not mean you build it once and leave it to rest. It means you build it (the plumbing) once, leverage the analytics to enhance it, and continually improve it based on data. You are making it more robust for that rainy day when you need to enter a new market or you bring in a new cohort of baby users. The race is to customer centricity, period.

Transforming your transformation means using data to lead you. The insights need to drive what you build and, as mentioned previously, based on a value framework. The key here is not around how much content is being built but how much of the DAP functionality is being leveraged and how often.

Think about the real estate by the checkout counter in a supermarket. The first step is to appreciate that there is space that can be monetized. As a result, some display units are placed in that space. This is the plumbing.

Then we add the chocolate bars (guidance), then the visible signage around the magazines (engagement), and perhaps some prepaid retail cards (smart tips). This is the dressing on top of the plumbing. Over time you will figure out what sells (works) and what doesn't all based on the sales (business outcomes).

Now logically, you would then react to the data. This is the refresh part of the process.

We know that people use different content in different contexts. They may be at different parts of the process or have familiarity with the process. They may need some guidance or validation. Perhaps they need more information so being able to search, find, and leverage resources may be important. In some extreme circumstances you may be dealing with what I describe as a reactive user; you know that person who ignores all your advances, emails, phone calls, etc.

With a DAP, you can segment your content to proactively get in the face of a reactive user. Think about it, no more chasing up Raj-type users ever again. Now overlay this with a new user vis-à-vis a veteran. Context is incredibly important.

To keep up with context, organizations should consider a way to benchmark the quality and recency of the DAP content. A DAP provides a range of functional elements; guidance, engagement, automation, validation, segmentation, resources, et al., and these functional elements when blended enhance the solution offering but also helps to refine the business outcomes you are looking for. We discussed this in "content is king."

The challenge is how to keep your team honest. One way to do this is to create an adoption score index. This is a holistic single metric that tries to represent what good content looks like. It takes the functional elements that the platform provides, identifies the elements used in the content build, and applies a weighted average.

Some elements may carry more weight, such as automation, because we know, based on the science of adoption, that by removing the empty clicks in a process you effectively slice the time to completion in half while also enhancing completion rates. Some estimates suggest that, through automation, a DAP has helped employees save over 154 hours a week. The adoption score in this case represents the value you are getting from the DAP at that point in time.

The score improves or declines based on two variables: A) how much more relevant content is built, and B) how often. To get to this you simply rely on the insights engine of the DAP platform.

So, for new ways of working to truly come alive, you will need a powerful insights engine. It's a great mechanism to keep your internal DAP team (SWAT team) honest and competent.

The DAP is not a replacement for your digital transformation program. It is the enabler. Your strategy is likely to be sound. It is the execution that may be spotty, leading to employee or customer frustration, not to mention possible speed bumps in your share price

Investment

As part of rethinking your business and transforming it digitally, you will need to rethink your organization's attitude toward its overall DAP strategy. You will need a DAP strategy and once you get to this point, then the building blocks around content, org structures, etc., will naturally be questions you know you will need to address.

Hopefully, at this point you will not make the mistake of thinking of content as mere words on a page when, in fact, your content is so much more than that. It's a valuable, monetizable asset.

Think of it this way: Would your organization make a big investment in software, hardware, or even physical infrastructure without maintaining it? Would they buy it and just leave it alone? Of course not.

Instead, your organization should treat it as a performing asset, maximizing its usefulness to achieve your desired business outcomes. This is exactly how your organization should approach its DAP content.

For instance, what DAP content do you update? You won't know unless you have DAP insights. The analytics will tell you that people are engaging with your content, say, 60,000 times. That's extremely important and confirms what's working.

But what if you build something and no one is using it? There will be a few possible reasons: The users don't need it, it's broken, or they don't know about it. But how will you know? Your DAP can tell you. Once you know, how will you fix it? Again, your DAP content will be the solution for your solution.

To be fair, there isn't a hard-and-fast rule around how often business leaders should be looking at the insights a DAP provides. It comes down to whether you see your DAP driving a new way of working.

At a strategic level, the CIO may want visibility into what applications they have deployed, how much usage there is and may well try to quantify the value of the investment vis-à-vis the usage. Being able to see what that looks like over a month, a quarter, or a year would prove useful.

An operations manager who tracks the average handling time of calls may leverage insights on a daily, weekly, or monthly basis to understand if there are opportunities to drive greater efficiencies into their operators' days.

Or there is the program owner who is trying to drive completion of time-sensitive processes like goal setting or zip code updates who need daily and weekly visibility.

The key here is having the ability to have those insights to act.

Operational Mindset

The whole notion of digital transformation means change. Your organization is changing digitally to solve a business problem. But if your day-to-day operations remain the same, then it's not really a transformation.

You may be transforming the veneer of your company but not the guts of it. Essentially, you're slapping a fresh coat of paint on your organization, one that will soon fade, and your organization will be in trouble once again.

Allow me if you will, a sports analogy. In American football, much is made of two types of offensive philosophies. There are teams whose offensive philosophy is primarily running (rushing) the ball, while others hold to an offensive philosophy of primarily throwing (passing) the ball.

Now if the rushing team wants to become a passing team—meaning it plans to succeed by transforming from an old way of working to a new one—it requires much more than a change in philosophy. The team can't just say, "We were a rushing team but now we have transformed into a passing team," and it's done. They really have to transform. And not just how they play the game, but they also need to transform their assets.

Adopting that philosophy is only the first step. Next, they have to take the steps to live their new philosophy. This means having coaches who understand how to plan and strategize for a passing team. It requires finding or training players with the skills to put this new philosophy into practice.

It's the same for your organization's transformation. You can't simply say you're transforming from one way of working to another and it's done. You have to take a holistic look at your leaders and employees and train them to put your new philosophy into practice in daily work.

Having a DAP, to extend the sports analogy, is like having a coach whispering in your player's ears as they play the game, making suggestions, telling them what they need to know when they need to know it, reminding them of all their tasks, etc. And having the data is like an eye in the sky telling the coach which calls to make and when, telling players where to go and what to avoid.

Notice I'm not saying that your organization wants to go from being a football team to a baseball team or a basketball team. You're only trying to transform how you play, from a rushing to a passing team. And the reason you're trying to transform how you play is that when you suddenly realize that your competition has built a team to counter your rushing (operational) philosophy. But you also realize they don't have the flexibility and the agility to be able to counter a passing team.

So, you're trying to figure out how quickly you can pivot from a rushing to a passing team, or more importantly, be able to do both with the same personnel. If you can do both with the same personnel, you'll have distinct economic advantages. You don't have to go get a different type of coach and different types of players. It's like having a rushing quarterback or a passing quarterback that can do a little of both. That's tough to defend against.

Three Types of Resources You'll Need

If you're truly going to reap the benefits of a digital transformation, you will need to rethink the delivery of the experience from beginning to end.

In the football analogy, if we were to shift from a rushing to passing game, there are a few roles that we may need to bring in. In the passing game, the quarterback becomes more critical because he needs additional seconds to search out his target. Now if he were right-handed, his left side periphery vision would be blocked. This is where a left tackle (position) becomes a critical addition. Below are three types of "players" you will need to leverage a DAP for a successful digital transformation.

You will need three resource types (depending on your scale):

1. DAP Consultant: This is your DAP subject matter expert who understands what the platform functionally can do. This is the go-to person who will build your content.

2. DAP Program Manager: Remember it is about building assets that solve a business problem. This role requires the individual to lead cross-functional teams through the content curation process. This includes the design, build, and managing of the platform including the analytics.

3. DAP Strategist: A strategic role once you shift your thoughts from solving tactical program issues to trying to build content that can drive cashable benefits, as a result, improving the value-driven from tech-dependent investments.

These may be additions to your team, or they may be current team members who train to take on these roles. By investing in these resource types, your organization will gain the flexibility of being able to change the user experiences that will help you arrive at different business results. What is key is this, to get different business results, you need to have different behaviors.

To induce different behaviors, you must understand the belief system of human beings. We all fundamentally want to know, "What's in it for me?"

If your people don't believe they will benefit from your transformation, they won't come on the journey. But if you could make the technology journey more human (which is what a DAP is all about), knowing where someone needs assistance, when they need it to get them back to their day jobs, then maybe we would be able to bend the curve on value realization. Your user sees what's in it for them.

The next step is to translate beliefs into experiences. As you go through your transformation and create those human-like experiences, it will lead to different, more positive, actions.

When you look at turning beliefs into experiences, think about how people experience the world. How many leaders have sat in the seat of the front-line operator? Try it out for a day and you will begin to understand how experiences matter.

Take the humble automated teller machine. Before the ATM came about, you typically needed to line up in a branch, fill out a withdrawal slip and stand in line before completing your transaction with Marge, the teller. Marge would ask you for some identification, she would ask you some questions and you probably would exchange some pleasantries. After that tango, she finally hands over your money. This ritual could take as long as anywhere from two minutes to 45 depending on how long the lines were and how many teller windows were open, etc.

Two weeks later you come back to do the same thing, but you see a new machine. The instructions say, "Insert ATM card, key in your PIN, and state the amount of money you need."

You say you want 100 bucks. You get the money. You get a receipt. You go on your merry way after a transaction that takes you at most three minutes.

With an experience like that, which would you run to the next time? The ATM, of course. Why? Because you've realized it benefits you. You've cemented that with experience. You've connected. Now, if you had to take a four-hour training course on how to use the ATM, I am not sure that connection would be as strong.

This connection between belief, experience, and action is what I mean by a new way of working. Any new way of working is going to require people to understand the new way of working. The DAP content is how you ensure they understand.

Use a DAP to transform your business—changing the way your organization thinks and the way your people work—and you'll find the rewards of a true digital transformation go far beyond even what you're initially hoping for when you set out on your journey of transformation.

Scope and Scale

Over time, your biggest DAP challenge will be one of scope and scale of content. Your DAP content should grow continuously, as existing processes will need improving and new processes will need to be incorporated. The analytics will highlight new friction points. The content may need to be translated to support a new market entry. The organization may need to pivot at a moment's notice and by leaning on your DAP and content as a service ideology your ever-changing baby user population will have a support mechanism ready and waiting.

As your time using a DAP goes on, you'll notice something curious happening within your organizations: the farther away you get from a piece of content's creation and the core team who created it, the harder it becomes to maintain that content.

The people who created the content (who ideally are the same people who use the content, remember) will move into other roles within your organization or to other organizations completely. New people will replace them.

The new baby users won't have a bond with the DAP. They won't share the same sense of ownership and passion for the DAP content as the superhero users they replaced. As such, the new baby users—while themselves becoming superusers—may not be as diligent about keeping the content current. They may not offer suggestions for new content or processes to be incorporated into the DAP. Heck, the new people might not even realize they have a say in what the DAP content should be.

And this is because the farther your DAP and its content travel from its point of origin and into the hands of people who didn't create it, the farther it also gets from how it ties to the strategic initiatives that lead to the DAP in the first place. So, you must have a plan or strategy around content as an asset. Who owns the asset? You will need accountability for this to work.

De-risking Your Strategic Programs

Every organization will have three, maybe four strategic programs that all employees are compensated on. These programs attract plenty of funding but also much scrutiny. These sexy programs can be career-enhancing for superheroes or limiting. These could be the launch of a digital bank or an ERP transformation—both having a fundamental impact on the P&L.

I should mention one more superpower a DAP can give to your organization: de-risking. Because a DAP gives you so much detailed information on the friction spots in your processes and organization *and* it gives you the simple tools to rapidly smooth over those spots, your organization can minimize the draining of costs and resources.

This allows leadership to not only shore up existing processes but allows them to continually rethink and optimize the business with the confidence that any changes can quickly be assessed and adjusted as needed. It's as if, extending the metaphor, organizations attain the innovation velocity of a superhero who counts speed as one of their competitive superpowers.

Organizations can innovate at pace and scale. Leaders can leap forward with new initiatives in greater numbers and at an increased pace because they're confident their DAP will help them quickly identify and resolve unforeseen friction spots in any new process or system. Additionally, because the DAP allows both baby users and leaders to learn while doing, the time it takes to try, refine, and expand new initiatives is cut dramatically.

You need to be able to link your strategic programs. For example, it might be something like frontline obsession. Right now, a lot of CEOs' number one issue is frontline obsession, which is another way of saying, "Be obsessed with the customer (or user) experience." That's great, but what technology-dependent investments are they making to enable that frontline obsession? How are they measuring the operational needs around it? And how is that tied to cashable benefits? You have to answer those types of questions to do the necessary work of linking strategy with operational excellence and ground-level execution. Only then will you be able to assess the return on your investment in your digital transformation.

Once you have been able to de-risk your program, the focus can shift to accelerating and maximizing the original business case promises. You must pause and be able to explain how you are de-risking the tech dependencies of your strategic initiatives; how this deliberate strategy is impacting both operational and financial goals positively. Remember, you are always solving for "how."

It's in this way that a happy superhero baby user leads to an organization of superheroes performing at such a high level that leadership is encouraged to make bolder decisions to maximize the business. In turn, this leads to greater profits and greater pay for individuals in the company, who are then motivated to push their abilities even further on behalf of the organization.

And it all starts with leveraging the happiness of the individual baby user to make them into a hero.

DAP Dos

Ask yourself a simple question: Can you articulate the business issue you are looking to impact?

It doesn't need to be complex. Keep it simple. For instance, "We need to reduce the top 20 percent of support tickets on Application X or Y from 1,000 to 500 within 180 days."

If you have, terrific!

Now ask yourself:

Have you been able to measure that business objective accurately?

Now ask yourself:

How you are measuring the impact?

Do you have success criteria that you can look to?

How much visibility do you have on your digital transformation program?

How much of your information or feedback is anecdotal?

How precise can you be on how your tech investments are impacting your operational and financial goals?

If it takes you a week or a month to directionally know where you are, you may want to explore how a DAP can help lift the lid of mystery surrounding your program.

PAYBACK:
CASH IN—CASH OUT

C an we accelerate the payback on our tech investments? How do we take advantage of intangible benefits and drive operational and financial metrics in the transformation?

There will come a time—three at least—when you have to stand before your money men, colleagues, your team, and possibly even your shareholders to justify your digital transformation, including your decision to use a DAP to ensure the success of that transformation.

By justify, of course, I mean to make the business case for how all this change pays for itself. Oh, and how soon it does so. It's all about accelerating the payback period of those strategic technology investments.

The first time will be when you propose your sweeping, work-altering project. Then again as you're working within your organization to implement your vision. And, finally, when the time comes to settle up, look back, and see if you realized a return on your investment.

As I mentioned in Chapter 6, Forrester Research conducted in-depth ROI research across four different organizations (Red Hat, Inc., CHRISTUS Health, Modernizing Medicine, and Engie) that offer us some tantalizing results.

According to the report, these four organizations reported several benefits including reduced training time (60 percent), IT Help Desk savings (50 percent), and savings in software licensing fees (20 percent).

Forrester's analysis confirmed a 368 percent ROI in a payback period of less than three months with a present value of benefits exceeding $20 million over three years.[109]

As I said, tantalizing numbers. At the risk of sounding like a Business 101 course, I want to make a clear distinction among ROI, business cases, and the various types of benefits they measure.

ROI vs Business Cases

Always an interesting discussion but the business case typically lays out the case for the investment. Many of these cases are focused on improving capital efficiency where the investment appraisal looks to cashable and non-cash benefits over a payback period.

When an organization looks to the overview of benefits, they look to things like de-risking and accelerating and maximizing revenue targets, increasing application usage and efficiency, mitigating an increase in training and onboarding spend. Some will look at planning to mitigate IT support calls or help desk tickets whilst others will include the cost of decommissioning legacy platforms.

In short, the business case is the reason to make the investment. The ROI is the measurement of the benefits realized against the cost of the program.

Depending on the organization there may be four different types of benefits to think about:

1. Cashable financial benefits: these are benefits that generate an increase in revenue or savings so budgets or unit costs can be reduced.

2. Non-cashable financial benefits may not provide immediate savings to budgets although they may improve the quality of output.

109 "Forrester Analysis Found a Three-Year 368% ROI with WalkMe." 2020.

3. Risk impact to the program.

4. Business impact on the company.

Before you get to ROI and business cases, you may want to set the context for your audience. It's a good idea to clarify the stakes your organization is facing by answering two sides of a powerful question:

What are the implications of doing our DAP-driven digital transformation?

And, perhaps more importantly,

What are the implications of not doing it?

If you want to really drive home your point, break down that last question into several parts; how does a DAP help with:

Implications for your customers (must always be number one on this list)?

Implications for your increasingly decentralized organization?

Implications for your share price?

Implications for leadership's tenure?

Implications for employees in the time of overwhelmed employees?

Once your audience grasps the stakes, you may find everyone more receptive to examining the financial costs and rewards through an appropriate lens for the absolute need for a DAP.

Cash Flow, Cash Flow, Cash Flow

Financial metrics are a universal language. It doesn't matter if you speak Japanese, French, English, or Klingon, all companies understand discounted cash flow and internal rate of return. Cash in. Cash out. Reducing payback. These are the fundamentals that cut across businesses, industries, cultures, and geographies.

The key question is if your digital transformation or investment is going to impact cash coming in or going out? Is the DAP going to reduce the tech-dependent business risk or accelerate the pace of execution by bringing forward the payback period of the tech investment? Will the DAP help to maximize the returns of the tech investments?

If you think about the current business-as-usual state, organizations typically buy software, build out platforms and solutions, go live, get through the hyper-care phase of training and support, and then move on.

The success of the rollout is typically measured at go-live or at hyper-care. To get a more accurate reading on its success, we need to measure whether we have de-risked operation and financial goals, accelerated the payback period of the tech investment, and whether we can measure how we continue to maximize the value realized from the program. This is where a DAP plays a critical part, but it requires rethinking our current ways of working.

Which brings us back to ROI and the business case for your DAP-driven transformation. Both ROI and business case measurements quantify aspects of your DAP-driven digital transformation. But in some ways, ROI and business cases are very different aspects of business measurement. The distinction between the two holds the key to accurately and thoroughly measuring the effectiveness of your organization's DAP-driven digital transformation.

ROI is basically a question of, "What did we get for our investment?" That is, there is a dollar amount that goes into every investment. How did the end financial result do against that dollar amount?

Business cases are built around those four benefits highlighted above. Your business case is tied to the payback period of the technology investments you're making to drive the strategic initiatives within the organization.

That seems pretty straightforward, but there are two real facets you need to think about. The first and easy one is *cashable benefit*.

What is a "cashable benefit?" Simply put, cashable benefits are changes that will "directly reduce an organization's budget either through savings or through additional revenue."[110] For our purposes (assessing the effectiveness of our DAP-driven digital transformation), it is any cash-specific benefit related to our project that goes in or out of our business. Change the cashable lever and the result is pretty straightforward (open to let more flow in, close to restrict flow out).

As for the intangibles' benefits, while they're easy to understand, people often miss what's truly important—their implications for the business. Consider productivity. Just because someone's more productive doesn't necessarily mean they are impacting cash in and cash out. It's an intangible, non-cashable benefit. For now, anyway.

Here's a tangible, real-world example of what I meant. Walgreens set out to improve customer experience by improving employee experience.[111] That meant eliminating unproductive work, reducing employee frustration, and giving employees the space to help customers. That all sounds good, but is intangible. How can that be viewed in terms of cashable benefit?

By addressing back-office processes to free up time for the employee, those employees were able to spend more time on the shop floor helping customers. Walgreen's internal metrics showed both correlation and causation between time spent on the floor helping customers and increased revenue.

That's how an intangible becomes aligned with the tangible benefit it helps create.

So, when you provide a platform, like a DAP, that enables people to be more productive, you need to translate that increased productivity into something meaningful in terms of generating revenue or reducing costs:

- Revenue that can be measured as a cashable benefit to the company
- Or reductions that can be measured as a cashable benefit to your business

In that way, an intangible like productivity is tied to the very tangible

---

110 "Benefits Realisation Management Framework, Part 5: Glossary," New South Wales Government, 2018, 6, https://www.nsw.gov.au/sites/default/files/2020-11/brmf%20glossary.pdf.

111 Mark Wagner and Wayne Orvis, "Changing Structures and Behaviors at Walgreens," *Strategy+Business*, no. 72 (Autumn 2013), https://www.strategy-business.com/article/00195?gko=ba7e8.

cash benefit. Doing that—showing how to *attribute* the intangible benefits' impact on cash in and out of the business—arms you with a credible
narrative showing why your project is important.

For instance, you could put a DAP on top of your processes that improve productivity in your organization. This isn't necessarily a cashable
benefit. But if being more productive leads to an increase in sales or reduction in costs that you can attribute to the improvement in productivity,
then this is terrific. The key is being able to tie the impact to the improved
outcome. Can you clearly attribute the impact to the DAP?

If I was able to increase the number of quotes I could get out to prospects given an improvement due to the DAP by 50 percent which led to
a 25 percent increase in sales or an additional $100,000 in revenue, this is
a cashable benefit that we can attribute to the productivity gain. Without
the DAP, that increase in volume and improvement in revenue would not
have occurred, hence it's "attributable." Better still if a strategic objective
of the organization was to increase revenue by X percent, then the DAP
has just impacted the P&L and become relevant to the board's objectives
for the year.

With your DAP, you'll solve the individual problem along with all the
other process challenges that are costing your organization time and, yes,
money in a multitude of areas. It's what you do with the time that matters,
along with whether or not you can tie it to a cash benefit. Critical here is
the evolution of the role played by your financial analyst. Programs will
need access to this skill to help with the math associated with the internal
rate of returns and discounted cash flows.

Let's say you saved somebody from having to sit through classroom
training for five days per year. You've also reduced the amount of time that
a trainer has to conduct training classes. You've been able to free up time
so people can do other revenue-generating tasks. All of that is a qualitative,
quantifiable benefit as opposed to a cash benefit. You may be saving someone time, but you're not reducing your salary costs.

Now here's a cashable benefit from using the DAP: Let's say that as a
business, one of your strategic growth objectives is to enter or accelerate

growth in a new market or markets. In your approved business plan, you have made provision for increasing the number of trainers from 40 to 80. Now if you build DAP content, specific to the system training elements you find that you only need an additional 20 trainers and not the original 40 as budgeted. If each trainer were to have cost $100,000 a year in salary (cash out), you would have avoided spending $2 million (cash out). Now that's a real impact from using a DAP.

Or let's look at recruitment from a different angle to get to a cashable benefit. Let's say it takes an average time of 45 business days to hire a new employee. That's nine weeks if you divide it by five business days.

Let's assume that the impact an employee can have when on the job is $10,000 a week (five business days) in additional revenue. Every week you manage to slice off your hiring process time is an additional $10,000 you bring into the company. If you can reduce the time to trigger the hiring process, make it easier for people to navigate the process once it's initiated and ease any friction points lurking in the end-to-end hiring and training process, you're gaining cashable benefits. Hiring managers and recruiters all understand the significance of reducing the time-to-fill roles, especially revenue-generating roles but now with a DAP, the implications of the cashable benefit become very real.

Now ask yourself this question, "Can we solve these types of questions today with our current operating model?" If you can't, it might be time to reassess how you are de-risking your transformation program.

The Hidden Importance of Soft Costs

At first glance, executives often dismiss the benefits of a DAP as "soft" (qualifiable) versus "hard" (quantifiable or cash) benefits. But the "soft" stuff turns out to be quite important because of the implications it can unlock; and when you can unlock these, they become pure gold.

To see how that happens, let's expand our example: You've got 5,000 people and you're rolling out a bunch of new technology as part of your digital transformation. You're going to have to train all 5,000 people. And let's say each of them has to learn ten new things on an application. That's now 50,000 new things to be learned in aggregate terms.

Let's say it'll take 10 minutes to learn each of these things. Now you're at a total of 500,000 minutes of training. Divide that by 60 and you're looking at a collective 8,300 work hours to get all your people up to speed. And please don't forget our good "friend," the forgetting curve.

Now some detractors are going to say, "We wouldn't necessarily train all our employees for all the processes." But the reality is that most employees will probably spend 10 minutes or more searching for support material, then reading and digesting it, perhaps looking and asking for help. So, whilst the formal part of the training or learning may never have taken place, the informal part as you can see would certainly take precious time away from the execution of the process. The key again is how do we tie this back to a cashable benefit. Let's see how we can attribute this to the process.

Let's go ahead and multiply that by $20 an hour. That's about $166,000. This is the opportunity cost for training taken from a salary perspective. That is, it's the cost of simply taking someone out of their day job and sticking them in a classroom.

But if you deployed a DAP, you wouldn't have to put people through all that training. They wouldn't have to go to the classroom to be trained. You wouldn't have to take them out of that environment. And those 5,000 people could just reach out for help when they need it in the flow of work just like you would the GPS in your car; when you get lost, need a gas station, to check on traffic. The aim is to create an end-user experience where change management effectively gets reduced to almost zero at day one.

Now when you look at it properly, that opportunity cost of $166,000 is an absolute qualifiable, qualitative measurement. It doesn't have a direct impact to cash in or out. The *aha!* moment should be that you can use your DAP-driven digital transformation to create and enable new ways of working where the original 8,300 minutes get translated into real revenue generating or cost reduction activities.

When COVID-19 hit, the immediate win was remote access for employees. The fundamental question was, "Can our employees access the systems we and they need to in order to execute on tasks critical for their day jobs?"

Access was the focus, rather than the inability to use the applications or consistently completing the processes. Consistency is going to be WFH 2.0 because working from home is our new reality. This is where DAP can and will be the key differentiator.

The initial heavy lifting was around enabling your large workforce to work from home. That in and of itself isn't a cash benefit but the implications can be. Maybe you are able to slice a significant percentage of real estate costs given the new work from home policy. This could be quite profound. You no longer have to house people, pay for electricity, provide parking, feed people, etc. All these items impact the P&L. These are real cash benefits.

The New York Times reported in April 2021 that many large companies, such as JP Morgan Chase, Ford Motor Company, and Target are giving up expensive office space because of the success of remote work. They are not alone. United Airlines is giving up more than 17 percent of its space at the Willis Tower in Chicago. Salesforce is subletting half its space (approximately 225,000 square feet) in the iconic Salesforce Tower.[112]

Jamie Dimon, chief executive of JP Morgan Chase, suggested that for every 100 employees, his bank would only need approximately 60 seats because "the pandemic had proven that work from home is viable."[113]

This shift isn't restricted to the United States. In Singapore, Southeast Asia's largest bank, DBS Group Holdings, the world's most recognizable digital banking group announced a reduction of physical office space. They are contracting their office footprint by 75,000 square feet in Singapore in one building alone and have pared back their real estate footprint in Hong Kong as well.[114] In the UK, HSBC Holdings has announced that it is allowing its staff of 1,200 at its British call centers to permanently work

---

112 Peter Eavis and Matthew Haag, "After Pandemic, Shrinking Need for Office Space Could Crush Landlords," *The New York Times*, April 8, 2021, https://www.nytimes.com/2021/04/08/business/economy/office-buildings-remote-work.html.

113 Ibid.

114 Prisca Ang, "DBS to Cut Office Space by 20% In Next Few Years," *The Straits Times*, May 1, 2021, https://www.straitstimes.com/business/banking/dbs-to-cut-office-space-by-20-in-next-few-years.

remotely.[115]

Thanks to the flexibility of being digital and being able to work with digital tools, organizations have options that allow them to right-size their non-performing asset line items in the P&L. In time, I predict many retail banking sites will close as more and more services shift online.

Employee turnover is another place where cashable benefits emerge when viewed properly. Let's take that 5,000 employees and say you have a turnover rate of 10 percent a year. That means every year you have to train 500 new baby users to cover attrition. And that's just if you're holding steady. But you're not; your company is growing by 10 percent a year. That's another 500 baby users you're going to train to cover your growth.

This is where your DAP content becomes an important cashable benefit if you need to hire more resources to build content. If you have to train these 1,000 baby users (500 to replace turnover, 500 to keep up with growth) the traditional way, you're going to have your team of instructors build training content. Those trainers may have to build three, four, or even five different training assets. Those assets may bring in different media such as video, rather than being limited to text on slides. Each asset may take multiple days to build. By developing content on a DAP, these additional change network costs can be mitigated.

If you're a global organization, you're going to have to build all the training content in multiple languages.

But remember: you're working in this new world of ours where things are changing, updating constantly due to the cloud. Every time there's a change or an update, the trainers have to update all those training assets in all those languages.

Finally, let's be honest. You don't know for certain how many, if any, of those 5,000 employees ever sees or uses all the content built for them.

It's a costly (in terms of time spent) and inefficient process that, as we've discussed earlier, doesn't factor in our natural ability to forget things we just learned but seldom practice (here comes that pesky forgetting curve again).

---

115 Iain Withers and Lawrence White, "HSBC Moves More Than 1,200 UK Staff to Permanent Home Working," Reuters, April 7, 2021, https://www.reuters.com/article/uk-hsbc-working-from-home-exclusive/exclusive-hsbc-moves-more-than-1200-uk-staff-to-permanent-home-working-idUSKBN2BU1QH.

But with a DAP, you build all this content once and automatically refresh it in multiple formats. Not only does it adapt for you, but it also de-risks, because if or when your content creators disappear into new roles or companies, you already know where things are.

This same model and its accompanying benefits extend to your support center. Generally, you're going to receive two types of calls from your employees. The first is, "Hey, I don't know how to do this."

Which means you have to think about how you handle that call. How many times do people call with that issue? How long does it take you to solve that issue for them?

When you use a DAP to get the employees to self-serve, you're not reducing the need for the help desk. You're not reducing the head count. What you're doing is allowing your people to self-serve faster and so they and your help desk support staff can get back to their day jobs faster. Hopefully, as an organization, you will be able to accelerate your business outcomes faster. You are reducing the pressure on the help desk as it battles through its own challenges in retaining staff.

The second question your people usually call with is, "Hey, I'm in this thing and I don't know what format of data it needs. I keep getting an error message."

Using your content tool, you build some data validation rules into your DAP content that ensures the people are putting in the required information in the required format without having to take up time from your help desk staff, who are free to go deal with bigger issues. Again, you're not reducing head count and costs, but you are getting a better-quality outcome. These better outcomes will lead to better cashable benefits.

Getting Strategic with Your DAP

Ask yourself this simple question: "What would it mean to the business (and to me professionally) if we could improve the payback period of the technology investments we made around our strategic objectives by, say, three months, six months, a year, or two years?"

Most organizations start off a digital adoption project the first year with a few vital applications. That's enough to get you going in the right direction. Then, before long, you'll want to get strategic with your DAP. Now here's where you will really peel back the onion on costs and benefits.

You use your DAP strategically, tying its reach and content to the strategic corporate objectives. Within those objectives, you have targeted such categories as head count, investment in technology, investment in physical assets, and any other aspect of the business you choose to impact. These strategic investments or objectives were designed to either take advantage of a market or product opportunity or defend against a competitive threat.

Here's a real-world example of what I'm talking about. CHRISTUS Health, the faith-based healthcare provider, used a DAP platform initially to reduce non-cashable benefits such as training and support. It wasn't until the team realized that the power of a DAP was to solve real cash problems.

They mapped the day in the life of a health care worker and found that they had challenges in remembering the multitude of codes that needed to be assigned to a patient's bill.[116] You see they had a revenue leakage issue which they only discovered when the nurses and finance team members collaborated. The customer-facing team simply didn't understand the revenue impact of certain codes not being included on patient records. They overlaid data validation rules from their DAP over their billing forms and the impact from the correct billing codes being included was quite profound.

Within a matter of weeks, they collected more than $1 million in additional revenue (now monthly).[117] Investing in a DAP was truly an investment that had an impact on cashable benefits to the company.

From the finance side of the house, think of the big picture this way: You have a standard curve. You draw a line right down the middle of that curve. Whatever is on the right side of that line is the moment you break even and start being profitable. On the left is everything in red. If you

---

116 "CHRISTUS Health Uses WalkMe Digital Adoption Platform to Roll Out Crucial Technology to Health Care Professionals," WalkMe, accessed May 19, 2021, https://www.walkme.com/customer-stories/christus-health/.

117 Ibid.

deploy a DAP correctly, you're not attempting to move or bend the curve. You're moving the line so that you're getting cash benefits a year or two years ahead of time.

Say you're a bank and one of your strategic objectives is to roll out a digital bank. Why are you doing it? Because in two years, local regulators are going to issue five more licenses for digital banks and you need to get ahead of that reality because there's an under-served, under-banked population.

Great—how are you measuring that?

Well, you need to be able to measure it in terms of revenue. You expect to go from $1 million to $5 million in revenue. You need to make sure your cost to acquire a customer isn't more than $50. You need your costs to serve and to innovate to be less than your cost to acquire new customers.

Plus, you've got your applications, your 10 different technologies people have to use to interact with your bank. And if you have friction at this point where customers and your bank interact, you'll never fulfill your promise. But if you can solve it with a DAP, you can meet and exceed customer expectations. A customer activates an account and gets a card from your bank. They spend $100 a month. Now you're able to accelerate that and multiply that by 5,000 or even 10,000 customers. In this way, you've accelerated the cashable benefit upfront.

That's what a DAP can do, from simple process problem-solving to turn baby users into superhero users to paying for itself many times over by helping your organization realize high-level, strategic objectives.

DAP Dos

Linking your corporate objectives with your operational and financial goals is standard practice for most companies. The theoretical exercise is simple enough to do but being able to quantify the impact of the technology investments made and being able to measure and attribute the impact to those metrics is difficult.

How do you do it today? Do you even do it today?

When working with my customers, I typically ask for the financial analyst who helped create the original business case to share the original metrics. I try to understand if we are on track. Or are there levers we can pull to accelerate more value?

Are you on track to deliver on your original promises? Or are they merely hopeful goals with no way of knowing if you're making real progress?

CHAPTER 11

THE DAP MOVEMENT

W e are in the middle of a digital revolution. Like all preceding economic revolutions, this digital revolution offers us the opportunity to impact humanity holistically. And yet, thus far, its impact has largely been aggravating.

At home and in the office, we have experienced unabating waves of change. Digital transformation has become our everyday reality. How we embrace, accept, and adopt new ways of working and living are synonymous with how we engage in the world.

But if digital transformation is meant to improve our everyday lives, it needs to do two things. First, it must serve as a key strategic pillar supporting society. Second, it needs to make our digital world accessible to every stratum of society rather than merely a select few.

I'm not overstating it when I say that digital adoption platforms are the great equalizer in our digital revolution. DAPs have the potential to deliver the promises of digital transformation to everyone in the world. I know this because I've experienced it.

I've witnessed firsthand how a DAP can transform global organizations from the inside and out, just like the caterpillar transforming into the butterfly. How it can make technology work for users of all socioeconomic backgrounds regardless of their comfort level with technology. There's no reason to think DAPs can't do the same for the world.

Make no mistake, the DAP movement has already begun. In the decade since being born out of a son helping his mother navigate an online banking transaction, DAPs have been quietly working their way around the globe. Regardless of geography, language, culture, or industry, this revolution shows no signs of slowing down. Movements gather pace and scale and judging by my air miles an acceleration is on the way.

As a display of my confidence in the potential for DAPs to change our world, I went so far as to do the unthinkable and include predictions in the introduction to this book. Yes, I am a true believer in the potential of DAPs.

The coming DAP movement is inevitable but, as I hope I've made clear, DAPs must be implemented with proper critical ingredients.

The first ingredient, without a doubt, is shifting to an insights-first approach to processes. This may sound logical and simple in theory, yet the complex reality of it means very few organizations can actually do this enterprise-wide. Without the ability to understand holistically how your tech investments are doing, you are simply in a situation where the blind lead the blind.

DAPs allow you a quantitative macro view on the use of your tech stack *and* allow you to zero in on root causes of friction. It's almost an X-ray lens where you can look below the skin to get a blow-by-blow understanding of the issue. As a result, you're better able to diagnose the problem and administer the right solution.

Second, for digital transformations to have a high impact on employees, customers, and the broader ecosystem, organizations need to shift to an outcomes-based digital transformation agenda. The boardroom conversation will need to shift from "What *and* why *are we doing XYZ?*" to a point where board members understand *how* a change will impact their business. Organizations need to realize this is an iterative process because no two customers are exactly the same. Keep thinking in terms of small wins.

Perhaps we might even see board members experience the transformations personally. They will come to understand that the functional benefits of technology only come alive when business problems are solved. And if the leaders haven't solved the problem, then all they've accomplished is placing yet another layer of complexity onto their problem. Leaders will understand that buying software and throwing it at the problem will not solve the problem. In fact, it only increased the challenges.

The truth is, it's easy to sell software. But experience is what helps you realize value. Leaders need to look for the experience in their vendors, bringing them into the fold to be partners in solving the value problem. The traditional vendor-buyer relationship needs to evolve to a collaboration between parties where experience benefits all parties and not just during the sales phase of the process.

Looking for the experience is one of a DAP's superpowers. DAPs give leaders the ability to see through the opaque layers of complexity within their organization's technology stack. And the level of visibility a DAP affords an organization is intimate.

For instance, you can build out diagnostic dashboards to understand a macro risk down to an elemental level of how your users are interacting with your tech stack. It allows you to understand the exact challenges you face on feature adoption as you add or update technology.

A DAP's visual analytic powers allow an organization to recreate actual experiences with process-discovery capabilities that help chart future process improvements. With a DAP, an organization can dissect every layer, every ingredient, and every reaction. This allows the organization to react with customized, personalized experiences that drive technology usage by employees and customers.

What I have just described is the beginning of the journey, not the end. Some of you reading this are saying, "Oh no, not another motherhood statement that's so far out of reach it fills everyone with anxiety."

I hear you. So, let's start with this simple question: can we improve employee satisfaction with our digital tools?

With a DAP, we can find your satisfaction baseline in tangible ways that unscientific employee surveys cannot.

Once we know where you're starting from, we can then use your DAP to zero in on specific applications. We can hone in on a specific process, or better yet a specific point in the process. With our DAP, we not only identify your friction points but also smooth over those points. We fix the actual problems.

After that, we'll use your DAP to take another employee check. Now that we have people happier in their jobs, perhaps our next aim for employee happiness is to shift from a five-day week to a four-day week.

That may bring us face-to-face with the question of how to reduce the friction points in terms of time to completion. Ultimately, we may not be able to shave off eight hours in a week. But if we get to four hours the outcomes will be amazing. You may have noticed that I haven't mentioned your P&L yet. The implications of what I've just described will flow upstream naturally.

This is what I mean by solving the *how*. By solving the *how* you begin to realize the goodness and richness of your technology investments. That goodness and richness drive operational and financial metrics which, in turn, will bend your NPV, DCF, IRR payback curves, or whichever metrics you use.

Remember, this is not hypothetical. I've seen it over and over in organizations. DAPs are a new way of working that makes it possible to drive true outcome-based results from your digital transformation.

Back to the big picture. DAPs can truly impact humanity on a global scale by democratizing who can participate in our digital revolution. This is where I think the real opportunity presents itself.

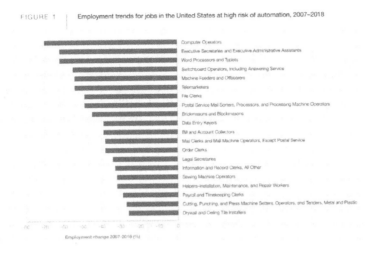

Figure 5: Employment Trends for Jobs in the United States at High Risk of Automation, 2007-2018[118]

DAP-driven new ways of working are going to impact employment trends. Again, to some degree they already have, and it's a movement that's growing.

Inevitably, we will see some types of jobs go the way of such once-ubiquitous jobs such as switchboard operator, mail sorter, and file clerk. But this doesn't mean doom and gloom to all people in the workforce. DAPs actually *provide* opportunities to the wider community of baby users rather than only for the technology savvy.

DAPs offer hope and opportunity to the disenfranchised. Had DAPs been around as the switchboard operator was being eliminated, it would have offered her the opportunity to shift into a call center role, allowing her to blend her skills with frictionless tech support. DAPs, in their purest form, democratize the use of technology.

Helping baby users to crawl, walk, and run in the decade ahead will determine if the digital revolution truly helps humanity. Digital leaders will be forced to decide: Are they going to sit by on the sidelines as their competitors transform? Or are they going to demand a new level of visibil-

---

118 "The Future of Jobs Report 2020," World Economic Forum, October 2020, http://www3.weforum.org/docs/WEF_Future_of_Jobs_2020.pdf.

ity through their tech stack to understand how they can improve the way their employees work?

In fact, they're going to have to come to see their employees *as* customers if they're going to compete for human resources. Digital consumers (including employees) will decide if the playing field they currently play on provides them with the best possible chance of economic, professional, and personal fulfillment. If their current playing field does not, they may very well pack up their toys and look for a DAP-driven field where they feel fulfilled with their ways of working.

What's more, DAPs offer hope to digital castaways. DAPs give those who feel left behind as work and the world have gone digital an opportunity to rise up and resurrect their careers. At the very least, DAPs are accessible for all. In the best cases, DAPs make work satisfying, too.

DAPs are changing the way we work and consume in a digital world. They are creating an entirely new industry. DAPs are turning digital castaways into baby users. Turing baby users into superhero users. Giving organizations the visibility into their processes to create happy customers and employees.

Digital adoption is as real as the sunrise is tomorrow. The question is: are you going to sit in the *what* and *why* chairs?

Or are you ready to be an active participant? Are you ready to embrace the power of *how* to transform our current digital revolution into what has the potential to be one of the greatest humanitarian efforts in the history of mankind?

The Power of How is Now.

AFTERWORD

I was inspired to write this book because of the data points I was confronted with from organizations, analyst reports, DAPs, and what each was teaching us. Over time, those insights have transformed into design principles. And while the data continues to evolve, the robustness of these emerging design principles will have a material impact on your digital transformation program.

Here are some examples of some of the design principles that have arisen:

- Do you know on average how many web forms your "customer" needs to traverse in order to complete that specific process?
- How long does it take them on average to successfully complete the process?
- (Not just do they make it, but how long and if they make it unscathed?)
- Do you know what the ideal time would be for a user to complete a process?
- Do you have data to highlight where the friction points are? Would easing the friction impact your business materially?
- On average, how many empty clicks does a user need to perform to get through steps in a process? How much time and frustration could be saved by automating these?
- Do you know the impact automation could have on your users as

they traverse your systems?

- Do you know the specific places where users need help? I let you in on a secret: in my experience the majority—higher than 75 percent, lower than 99 percent—of users don't need help at the start of a journey. They need it mid-flow. (Remember my trip to see my mum?)

- How are the completion rates in processes that have deep branching logic? You know, where there is a myriad of options, such as insurance claim forms, credit card applications, etc.

- Would overlaying support material within the application alongside specific fields in the forms reduce support costs? Do you know where these need to be placed in the flow of the process? Do you know who has used them? (Remember the Standard Chartered example?)

These are just some of the questions I would challenge you to think about and answer if we were sat across from each other. (FYI, I would be delighted to get into this robust discussion because it is material to the guts of the transformation that you have been trying to impact.)

To be clear, these questions are NOT mere hypotheticals. The initial data I have reviewed specific to digital processes in HR and CRM systems surrounding design principles is illuminating:

- Fifty percent of digital business processes are likely to fail if the time to complete the process exceeds 120 seconds.[119]

- Ideally, the data suggests that the time to complete a process should be 70 seconds. The data sees a 70 percent success rate for users.[120]

Now, if a process requires 10 steps or more, the data suggests that 50 percent of users are likely to fail. The ideal number of steps for completing

---

119 "WalkMe Unveils Unprecedented Data Highlighting Where Employees Struggle in Business Processes," Cision, April 10, 2019, https://www.prnewswire.com/news-releases/walkme-unveils-unprecedented-data-highlighting-where-employees-struggle-in-business-processes-300829801.html.

120 Ibid.

a business process is five steps, with a 70 percent success rate for users.[121] Your questions here should be, "How do we shrink the length of our processes?" The answer to that question lies in automation. The same data set found that users are 65 percent more likely to successfully complete a process with automation. A completion rate of 81 percent was verified, compared to 49 percent by non-automation users.[122] Not only does automation increase completion rates, but it also enables a higher chance of success for longer more complex processes (three times longer).

To get started I recommend you do the following: *agree on what is driving your digital transformation.* Many organizations make the mistake of letting technology solutions be their guiding principle or allow it to assume control. But here's what happens when you let technology solutions—rather than the business outcomes you should be seeking—drive your decisions.

Typically, organizations start by buying core technologies to digitize or automate processes. For instance, you want to transform your end-to-end sales process. You may start off thinking all you need is a CRM. But very soon you may be inundated with requests for a digital signature application or territory planning tool. Then you reactively plug any functional gaps in these core technologies with additional technologies intended to handle other parts of the sales process. Before you know it, you end up with six, eight, or 12 applications. It's not about the number of applications but rather about adding them reactively based on their promise.

ALWAYS REMEMBER: Plugging gaps in functionalities does not transform an organization. Solving business problems, like driving down SGA expenses or accelerating revenues, need to be your focus.

You may have already made the above mistake. Don't worry, you are not alone. It's not too late to save your digital transformation. Now that you know the path to a successful, DAP-driven transformation, deploy your DAP to all your users. Configure it to observe how your tech stack is being used. You don't have to build any content. All you need to know is what

---

121 Ibid.

122 Ibid.

technology you have deployed and how people are using it (or not using it). *Open the DAP systems dashboard a week later.* You'll be able to see how many users have accessed any specific application and how long they used it.

Congratulations, you are now up and running!

There is no need to overcomplicate your first baby steps. Keep true to what you are initially solving for (visibility) and let the data continue to grow. This will trigger a multitude of questions:

> *How many software subscriptions per application did we buy?*
>
> *Does 30 percent usage over 90 days constitute a good outcome?*
>
> *How much did we pay per subscription?*
>
> *Do we see applications with absolutely no usage?*
>
> *Can we terminate those agreements?*

And just like that, you are impacting the financial metrics of your organization. You're off and running in your DAP-driven world.

CPSIA information can be obtained
at www.ICGtesting.com
Printed in the USA
LVHW012030061021
699712LV00001B/2

9 789811 816499